9/11 Revealed

Challenging the facts behind the War on Terror

9/11 Revealed

Challenging the facts behind the War on Terror

Ian Henshall and
Rowland Morgan

ROBINSON
London

Constable & Robinson Ltd
3 The Lanchesters
162 Fulham Palace Road
London W6 9ER
www.constablerobinson.com

First published in the UK by Robinson,
an imprint of Constable & Robinson Ltd 2005

ISBN 1-84529-140-9

Printed and bound in China

1 3 5 7 9 10 8 6 4 2

This book is dedicated to the victims
of the events of 11 September 2001
and to activists of the 9/11 Truth Movement

Authors' Note

In what follows we do not seek to establish a definitive account of what happened on 11 September 2001, but rather to examine the official versions that emerged in the Autumn of that year and culminated in the publication of the Kean Commission Report in the Summer of 2004. We have also considered some but not all of the skeptical alternatives that have been presented by independent researchers, writers and experts. Given the state of the evidence it is clear to us that no one theory presented so far – official or unofficial – can be accepted as an uncontroversial account of what happened. It is entirely possible that Al-Qaeda conducted the attacks without outside help, and that the blunders that contributed to their terrible success were just that – blunders, as the Kean Commission's Report concludes. But as we show in the pages that follow, we do not feel that this conclusion can be treated as indisputable on the basis of the evidence so far made public.

Some of the alternatives outlined in the pages that follow may appear outlandish, even absurd, at first glance. Many of them conflict in crucial respects and at no point should we be taken to be advocating one over the others or over the official account. But cumulatively they amount to a serious case for the authorities in the United States to answer. If their version is correct they possess the evidence to put the matter beyond reasonable doubt. This evidence has not yet been produced. Until it is, we can only continue to insist that the most important single event in recent years remains an awful and unacceptable mystery.

Contents

Introduction

It is now over three years since the 9/11 events. But the collapsing towers, the smoldering Pentagon, the round sinister face of Mohammed Atta, still have an intense immediacy. Most people will always remember where they were when the news came through that hijacked planes had hit the World Trade Center and another was on its way to Washington. If some details of the day's events have faded, the mantra, "the world has changed", seems as relevant as ever, with the bloody occupation of Iraq and the steady erosion of citizens' rights in many countries.

In the crisis atmosphere anything seemed possible. A declaration from Bush on the morning of the attacks – without even time for a Cabinet meeting – that America was at war caused little surprise. Within weeks, any ideas that this was a figure of speech would be dispelled.

As the *Washington Post*'s Bob Woodward has put it, 9/11 was the defining of the Bush presidency. Bush got a free ride on the two scandals that emerged in the weeks after the attacks: the voter frauds in Florida, and the unravelling of Enron – whose managers had been among Bush's biggest campaign backers.

The study cited polling in the Arab world that revealed widespread hatred of the United States throughout the Middle East. A poll taken in June by Zogby International revealed that 94% of Saudi Arabians had an "unfavourable" view of the United States, compared with 87% in April 2002. In Egypt, the second largest recipient of U.S. aid, 98% of respondents held an unfavorable view of the United States.

A 2004 LA Times report showed that the Pentagon's warlike response to 9-11 had only served to supercharge Arab hatred of the USA.

In the UK, however, 9/11 led to the erosion of Tony Blair's moral authority, as voters recoiled at the deceptions of his dossiers on Iraq. In justifying the attack on Iraq Blair was insistent the 9/11 events had changed everything.

The first public reactions in Europe and America were of overwhelming shock and grief, but still many asked how Al-Qaeda had achieved such a spectacular coup. The generally accepted answer was the attacks were unimaginable, or as Blair put it, "unthinkable". How could the US defenses have been expected to cope with an inconceivable event? Moreover, Al-Qaeda was a truly terrifying opponent. As the spectacular collapses of the Twin Towers were repeated again and again on TV, pundits explained Al-Qaeda had millions – perhaps billions – of dollars and dozens, even hundreds, of sleeper cells across the US.

The world has indeed changed, but not entirely in the way expected. Within two years, majority opinion outside the US/UK would swing from seeing America as the world's victim to the world's bully. Internal criticism of Bush's America, for months only whispered, would become vociferous and commonplace with the bloodshed and allegations of systematic torture conducted by US forces in Iraq.

Iraqi Oilfields and Exploration Blocks

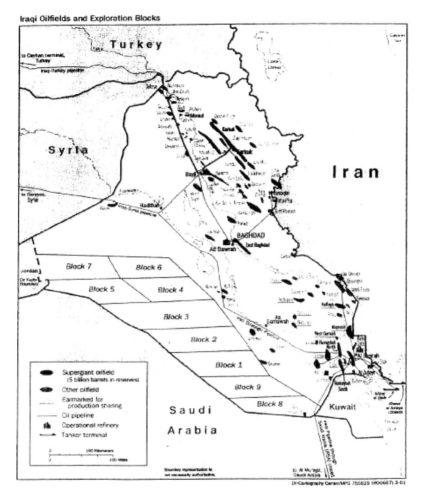

The map of Iraq drawn up by Dick Cheney's task force within days of Bush hijacking the 2000 election shows half the country sectioned "like a butcher's meat chart", according to Linda McQuaig. The claims are ready to be carved up by US Big Oil after the invasion, but Iraqi-resistance delayed privatisation. The map was released under freedom of information laws after a long struggle. Although the Iraq invasion (recruitment slogan 'Let's Roll' drawn from Flight 93's disappearance) was ascribed to Saddam Hussein's alleged links to the 9/11 events, the administration's prior war-preparation activities suggest that the motive was seizing the centre of the world's oil supplies.

Much has been written about the politics of the post-9/11 world and the Iraq war. But this book is not about that. This book is about a separate and arguably even more serious issue: is the official account of the 9/11 events even true? Nine/Eleven did not "change everything" simply because some violent people expressed their hatred of America, but because a number of these people had apparently acquired the *capability* of achieving mass casualties.

If Americans had thought at the time – as Thomas Kean's 9/11 Commission largely confirmed in 2004 – that the hijackers had been helped by the incompetence of the US authorities, the reaction might have been very different. But by 2004 mainstream America was beginning to ponder far worse possibilities than mere incompetence.

If Bush and Cheney were prepared to lie about Iraq's alleged weapons of mass destruction (WMD), and lie about Iraq's non-existent links to 9/11, were these same leaders prepared to lie about 9/11 itself? The official line has evolved from professions of shocked innocence to the tacit admission from the Kean Commission of a measure of incompetence. But the assertion that – against all the odds – Al-Qaeda just got lucky that day, is defended with the belligerent certainty – unsupported by facts – that has always been the hallmark of the official 9/11 story. There is no room for doubters. Questioning the official story has been equated with holocaust denial or – in a throwback to the Stalinist era – even with insanity.

We believe freedom requires the constant questioning of authority. Such is the long-acknowledged role of the media, the fourth estate. But it is a role they have abrogated, both over Iraq's alleged WMD and over the official 9/11 story. In this book we have gone back over the photographs and reports of the day, the warnings from foreign leaders and FBI agents, and the reaction – or lack of it – from the White House. We have examined how the evidence fits with the official story and with the alternative scenarios presented by the dissenters of the 9/11 Truth Movement. If there is reasonable doubt about certain key assertions of the official narrative, then inevitably the whole story is called into question.

The task of comparison is made easier now the Kean Commission has published a definitive version of the official story in the first thirty-five pages of its report. The US Government resisted all the way, but nearly three years later, the official story of the day is in print. President Bush welcomed it at the White House with smiles and back-slapping all round. When the official 9/11 narrative receives such endorsement, it is the duty of the fourth estate to take a close second look at the evidence.

The Background

1: The Official Story

Shortly after 8.46am Eastern Standard Time, US TV networks started showing live footage of the North Tower of the World Trade Center on fire. It had been hit by a plane, but at that time there was no film of the impact and many assumed it was an accident. But then, at 9.03, with many cameras now pointed at the buildings, a passenger jet hit the second tower.

It was now clear to all this was no accident: US targets were under attack. Within an hour, amid vague media reports of multiple hijacked airliners and a truck bomb at the Pentagon, spectacular pictures of the Pentagon's smoking and collapsed outer segment were presented to astonished viewers.

There would be hours of confusion before the exact details of what happened were officially agreed:[1]

- American Airlines Flight 11 took off from Boston's Logan Airport around 7.59am, was hijacked around 8.21, and slammed into WTC 1 – the North Tower.
- United Airlines Flight 175 was hijacked around 8.44am, and slammed into the South Tower.

- American Airlines Flight 77 took off from Dulles Airport, Washington, at 8.20am, was hijacked around 8.52, and flown into the Pentagon's only newly refurbished segment – still lying empty – at 9.37.

- United Airlines Flight 93, which had been delayed, took off from Newark, New Jersey, at around 8.42am, was hijacked at 9.28, and crashed in Pennsylvania on its way to Washington at 10.03.

But worse was to come with the total collapse of the Twin Towers: the South Tower at 9.59am and the North Tower at 10.28. Under each fire, the massive, so far largely undamaged, structures crumpled in less than twenty seconds into pulverized concrete, splintered steel beams, and a massive cloud of dust: providing an icon of biblical proportions for the first years of the new millennium.

Soon the TV studios received leaks from anonymous officials stating that the culprits were Arab hijackers from a sinister organization named Al-Qaeda. This, according to TV pundits, was controlled by a wealthy and hate-filled Muslim fanatic by the name of Osama bin Laden. Officials explained Al-Qaeda had succeeded so spectacularly as a result of great skill and a massively powerful organization. There had been no useful warnings, and the attacks had been, in any case, "unthinkable". This was Version One of the official story of the 9/11 events.

However, over the following months, under the radar of media commentators, a significantly different version of the official story took shape, let's call it Version Two. Version Two was published in 2004 by the National Commission on Terrorist Attacks Upon the United States, often referred to as the 9/11 Commission, and headed by Thomas Kean.

The Kean Commission conceded there were warnings that attacks might take place inside America, that they might involve hijacked aircraft, and that they would be directed at American symbols. There were many warnings of an imminent threat in summer 2001. And so, in Version Two, the problem was very different: senior officials, as they explained in anonymous briefings, failed to "join the dots".

If Al-Qaeda was ever a massively powerful organization (Version One), it was mostly disabled within weeks. By the time Osama bin Laden apparently escaped capture in December 2001, US officials were dismissing it as a spent force. In Version Two, the Kean Commission draws a picture of hijackers hard put to fly aircraft and lucky to evade detection, organized mainly by "freelance terrorist" Khalid Sheikh Mohammed.

In Version One, the failure to scramble US fighters to intercept the hijacked aircraft was due to inexplicably lost messages in the Pentagon. In Version Two, the Pentagon behaved faultlessly, but was hampered by extraordinary failures of air traffic controllers to pass on information.

Hailed as a triumph and nominated for the Pulitzer Prize, the Kean Commission's report[2] failed to deliver any answers at all on many glaring questions. How did the alleged hijackers gain visas on the basis of often grossly inadequate applications? Why did Mohammed Atta make an unnecessary flight to Portland, Maine, on the morning of the attacks – a flight that could have wrecked the whole project? Why were FBI officers forced to stop an investigation that might have aborted the attacks?

In addition, for many of its vital assertions, Version Two depends on evidence that cannot be tested: secret interrogations of alleged captured ringleaders in unknown locations and possibly involving torture; and radar reconstructions of the hijacked planes, supplied by the Pentagon. Vital witnesses – firefighters, FBI agents, and air traffic controllers – have been threatened with imprisonment if they give information to the public. Aircraft parts have vanished. WTC metal sections, which might have cast light on the unprecedented architectural disaster, have been sent unexamined for recycling.

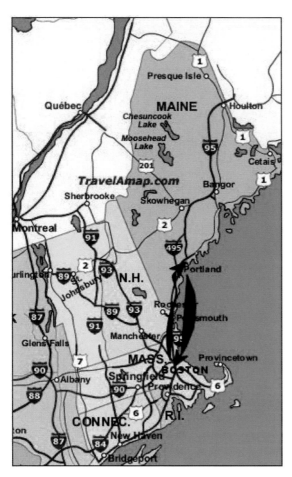

ATTA'S ROUTE TO PORTLAND AND BACK: The official story has Mohammed Atta leading the 9-11 attacks. But the Kean Commission admits that his connecting flight from Portland, Maine to Boston Logan airport on the morning of the events remains "a mystery". The puzzle: how could Atta have deliberately revealed his identity by the contents of his luggage, if he had no guarantee that the luggage would not be transferred to Flight 11 at Boston and destroyed in the WTC crash? Why, then, risk the whole operation by taking the luggage on a connecting flight at all? Perhaps Atta had an accomplice in baggage at Boston – but the FBI never investigated that possibility. For skeptics, the riddle brings into question the identity and motives of the alleged ringleader himself.

Credit: Based on TravelAmap.com

Before the days of President Bush and Vice-President Cheney, there was a saying in Washington: if you have nothing to hide, don't behave as if you have. Those days seem a long time ago.

Panic and War But No Inquiry

The initial shock subsided in the weeks after 9/11. But just when the first critical public questions might have emerged, a second threat paralyzed Washington. Anthrax attacks closed the offices of key senior Democrats and caused a general panic. The panic ended almost as soon as it had begun, with the revelation that the anthrax source was from a domestic military strain. Now was the time for the Washington media, trusted by most mainstream journalists on the planet as a source of truth, to ask the following question: given that the malefactor behind the anthrax attacks had tried to masquerade as an Islamic extremist, and given that the 1995 Oklahoma bomb had first been wrongly blamed on Islamic terrorists, could there have been a domestic element to the 9/11 events as well?

But by now it was two months after September 11 and the hot debate was over the Afghan invasion – war had overtaken truth in the media. What about Congress or the courts? On Capitol Hill Cheney strenuously opposed any inquiry. He privately lobbied Senate leader Tom Daschle, whose office had been targeted in the anthrax attacks.[3] Cheney's efforts ensured the most limited possible Congressional Inquiry, not into what happened in the attacks, but into the "intelligence failures" that were presumed to have contributed to them.

And what about apprehending the alleged perpetrator? Only 10,000 troops were sent to Afghanistan to pursue Osama bin Laden: fewer than the number of police in Manhattan. When the siege of the Tora Bora caves failed to capture the man named as the world's number one terrorist, US officials suggested he was, in fact, irrelevant.[4]

Meanwhile, with the failure to bring to trial any alleged senior Al-Qaeda operative, there was no opportunity to test accusations in court. Bush's decision that "enemy combatants" would be held effectively outside the rule of law stymied any judicial review of events, at least until a Supreme Court decision in 2004 qualified the new system. Not only the rights of the accused were denied but also the rights of the families of 9/11 victims – and indeed, the rights of people across the globe – to know the full story of the attacks.

Victims' relatives hoping for more information were confronted with a painful choice. Only if they agreed to waive their rights to take any legal action would they be eligible for the official compensation. The total pay-out was $6.9 billion, with more than 5,500 people receiving cheques averaging $2.1 million. By comparison, the victims of the Oklahoma bombing received roughly a tenth as much.[5]

The nearest to an official indictment of Al-Qaeda came not from the USA but from the UK Government, in the first of the now notorious Blair dossiers. Blair's Osama bin Laden dossier argued he had declared war on the US and several of the alleged hijackers were linked to Al-Qaeda. The Blair dossier did not investigate the extraordinary new skills displayed by Al-Qaeda, nor the obvious possibility that the attacks might have been helped by an outside agency in a "false flag" operation.

The official record of the 9/11 events was entirely based on facts asserted by the Washington intelligence establishment, and, in the days before the Iraqi WMD scandal, those without much knowledge of the intelligence world trusted the US/UK intelligence agencies to get basic facts right. Into a political atmosphere already poisoned by the Florida election wrangles had just entered mass murder, biological warfare, and war in Afghanistan. It was clear to journalists across the corporate media that this was no time to rock the boat.

The FBI's PENTTBOM investigation was apparently the biggest ever, covering over 500,000 leads and conducting over 165,000 interviews. In New York alone, over 1.8 million tonnes of debris were reportedly processed for victim identification and investigative leads. Like any criminal probe, its results were strictly secret but, uniquely, the government's case was never brought to court. As skeptic Eric Hufschmid put it, whilst describing the rigorously enforced ban on photographing debris at the WTC site: rules meant to preserve evidence for the courts were used instead to hide it from the public.[6]

Nine/Eleven skeptics have questioned how honestly the FBI investigation was conducted. Did it question the official story, or did it serve to "straighten out" the witnesses and select only the evidence that confirmed the government line? When investigator Daniel Hopsicker tried to talk to Mohammed Atta's girlfriend and associates in Venice, Florida, they said they had been warned not to talk to the media.

Other investigations should have taken place. The 9/11 disaster involved four crashed planes and three collapsed buildings, yet normal inquiries either failed to take place or were stymied by lack of information from the authorities. There was never an official air crash investigation. This was the first time in history even one steel-frame building had collapsed through any sort of fire, but fire chiefs complained that vital evidence concerning the towers' collapse had been destroyed when the steel was scrapped.

This left the field open to a range of investigations from outside the major US corporate media: independently owned and foreign newspapers and TV channels, corporate journalists turned freelance, curious professors, website editors, radical political groups, and individual internet news groups, contributors. The 9/11 skeptics have a wide range of views, the common thread being that there was some sort of US Government involvement in the attacks. Three million Deception Dollars were distributed by activists across America. The "Dollars", slightly larger than life, depict the President and are intricately adorned with the addresses of dissident websites.

Deception Dollars
Copyright: Blaine Machan (http://deceptiondollar.com)

It took time for word of mouth discussion, internet news channels, foreign news sources, and the few remaining independent US mainstream media to bypass the de facto censorship in Washington. But after the failure to find any of Iraq's promised weapons of mass destruction, a public that had rallied instinctively to its leader in September 2001 was questioning everything by 2004.

On the eve of the 2004 Republican National Convention in New York, the 9/11 Truth Movement commissioned an opinion poll by the respected Zogby organization.[7] The findings should have been headline news across America. As Zogby reported: "half (49.3 per cent) of New York City residents and 41 per cent of New York citizens overall say that some of our leaders 'knew in advance that attacks were planned on or around September 11 2001, and that they consciously failed to act'." Overall results have a margin of sampling error of +/–3.5. The percentages were particularly high amongst blacks, Hispanics, evangelicals, yet even 38 per cent of conservatives agreed. In a devastating verdict on the competence of the Kean Commission, 66 per cent called for a new inquiry into the "still unanswered questions" of 9/11.

Like the dissent of the anti-war movement, the dissent of the 9/11 skeptics movement has grown to astonishing proportions. But here the parallel ends. Many of the war's left-wing opponents are true believers when its comes to the official 9/11 story, and many 9/11 skeptics are on the conservative right wing. While the anti-war movement has enjoyed the sympathy of sections of the corporate media, editors have almost totally suppressed the question that should come first: do we need a "war on terror" at all? Is it credible that nineteen Islamic fanatics organized by Al-Qaeda carried out the 9/11 events without any help from certain elements within the US Government?

The War on Terror

If people on the left and in the peace movement were disturbed by the recourse to war for political reasons, 9/11 skeptics noted that the plans had been announced with suspicious speed, and they seemed to fit too conveniently into America's long-term goals. Washington and its allies were talking about a new world – but the response seemed to be straight from a more familiar agenda.

If there really were potentially dangerous countries cooperating with terrorists, they would most likely be nuclear-armed Pakistan and wealthy Saudi Arabia: but the White House was going after Afghanistan and Iraq. Britain's Paddy Ashdown is not known for his dovelike views. An ex-military man and a supporter for the bombing of Serbia and Kosovo in 1999, even Ashdown expressed surprise and concern at the "recourse to war".[8]

Bush and Blair seemed to move from the 9/11 events being "unthinkable" on day one to having a war plan virtually the day after. Lawyers, meanwhile, noted that the highly complex and detailed US Patriot Act must have been on the shelf waiting before the attacks took place. In a devastating leak in the wake of the Iraq war, ex-Treasury Secretary Paul O'Neil testified Bush had put Iraq top of the target list *not* in response to the 9/11 events but months earlier. This planning contradicts the media's assumption that the invasion of Iraq was a direct consequence of 9/11.

Could the White House have been waiting for the 9/11 attacks? Suspicions that officials did little to prevent them were finally confirmed in 2004 when, in another leak, White House anti-terrorism coordinator Richard Clarke said that national security advisor Condoleezza Rice and Cheney had virtually ignored the terrorist threat. After 9/11 Clarke was shocked to discover "with almost a sharp physical pain that Rumsfeld and Wolfowitz were going to take advantage of this national tragedy to promote their agenda about Iraq".[9]

War appeared in Bush's earliest comments on September 11. The President chose to declare the "war on terror" in the setting of Washington National Cathedral, arguably in defiance of the US Constitution, which reserves to Congress the right to declare war. This was no ordinary war either, it was to last, as Cheney put it, "beyond our lifetimes".[10]

Before the September 11 attacks, however, it was a given in international politics that war was not the way to deal with terrorism. Nobody proposed an invasion of Libya (then an ally of the IRA) when, in 1984, members of Her Majesty's elected British government were thrown from their conference hotel beds in the middle of the night by an IRA bomb, which wrecked a part of historic Brighton, killed two, and nearly killed Prime Minister Margaret Thatcher. For many of the world's citizens outside the thrall of the Western media, it looked as if 9/11 was the only terror attack that mattered; that American suffering was greater than anyone else's.

But the new war's proponents argued that – unlike the IRA or the old-style colonial liberation movements – the Al-Qaeda terrorists were madmen with no demands, who just wanted to destroy America, therefore negotiation was impossible. As if to underline the point, footage of celebrating Palestinians had been juxtaposed with photos of the falling Twin Towers again and again on American TV – it emerged later that the Palestinians were not celebrating the terrorist attacks but an unrelated local incident.

A video of Osama bin Laden was released, in which he denied participation in the 9/11 events and called for a US withdrawal from Arab lands and the dissolution of the state of Israel. However unpalatable, these were not the demands of a madman but the aspirations of millions in the Arab world and beyond.

For the 9/11 skeptics there was an equally troubling problem with the madman scenario. The presumed hijackers were bloodthirsty religious fanatics, but in this macabre sense the 9/11 events were spectacularly unsuccessful: about 54,000 people worked in the Twin Towers or were visiting during office hours, and fewer than 2,600 were killed or disappeared.[11] At the Pentagon there were over 20,000 staff, of whom 125 were killed or reported missing. If the hijackers had flown into the World Trade Center an hour or two later, or crashed into the roof of the Pentagon, instead of into the reinforced wall of an almost unoccupied segment, they could have killed thousands more of the enemy. But the good fortune that enabled the attacks to succeed ran out just as they reached their climax. For believers in the official story, if they noticed it at all, this was chance. For many 9/11 skeptics it was an indication the attacks had somehow been engineered.

Inquiries or Whitewashes?

By the time Thomas Kean's National Commission on Terrorist Attacks Upon the United States (otherwise known as the 9/11 Commission – or the Kean Commission) took form in 2003, most of the claims that created the 9/11 legend were still in doubt, but the legend had been polished by the corporate media for two years.

Cheney's strategy was successful: there has never been an official inquiry into who carried out the 9/11 events. There have, it is true, been two major probes, but they were into "failings" of the American defenses. They failed to ask whether the official story that emerged in a series of leaks during the panic of 2001 was correct. If they ever asked the obvious question – whether the massive, fiendish Al-Qaeda might have had informants within the US Government – it was not mentioned in public. The joint Congressional Intelligence Committee investigation in 2002 was held in secret, had poor access to official documents, and large parts of the final report were "redacted" (i.e. censored).

The Kean Commission should have addressed the issues raised in this book, but instead it serves merely as the bible of the official story. Its primary sources of information regarding crucial questions are classified intelligence reports and Pentagon radar reconstructions. Suspicious incidents are left unexplained, conflicts of evidence unresolved, and obvious questions ignored.

The White House took a long time to establish the Kean Commission. Finally responding to pressure from families of 9/11 victims, it first took the extraordinary step of appointing Henry Kissinger as chairman. Kissinger, who later became Secretary of State, made his name as an aide to disgraced President Richard Nixon in the Vietnam War. Kissinger stands accused of crimes from the bombing of Cambodia to instigating the 1973 military coup in Chile. After a storm of protest,

Kissinger, now a consultant, preferred to step down rather than reveal his sensitive client list, which included major oil companies.

The administration took care to prime the inquiry with a name – the National Commission on Terrorist Attacks Upon the United States – that pre-empted its conclusions. Philip D. Zelikow was appointed its executive director. He was close to Condoleezza Rice and had supervized the appointments process for the Bush administration.

Zelikow probably had better access to the evidence in his capacity as a Bush insider than he had officially as Commission director. For 9/11 skeptics, Zelikow represented a hot link from the Commission to the White House, should any problematic evidence emerge.

The "bipartisan" panel was stuffed with Washington insiders. Democrat Jamie Gorelick, for instance, wrote a crucial memo while she was at the Justice Department, which the Commission took to be the explanation for "intelligence failures". Senator Max Cleland objected to White House control of vital evidence: "This is a scam, it's disgusting. America is being cheated . . . We shouldn't be making deals."[12] He was soon replaced by Bob Kerrey, a member of the Committee for the Liberation of Iraq.

The Kean Commission Report does not just toe the official line. It is a gung-ho recruiting document designed to send the righteous to war: "We learned about an enemy who is sophisticated, patient, disciplined, and lethal. The enemy rallies broad support in the Arab and Muslim world by demanding redress of political grievances, but its hostility toward us and our values is limitless. Its purpose is to rid the world of religious and political pluralism, the plebiscite, and equal rights for women. It makes no distinction between military and civilian targets. Collateral damage is not in its lexicon."[13]

There is no room in this heavily charged passage for qualifications, such as the CIA's help in training Osama bin Laden when he first started out in armed politics.[14] This is not a world in which Donald Rumsfeld was once an ally of Iraq, shaking hands with dictator Saddam Hussein, or in which US intelligence had once keenly supported Islamic extremists.[15] Nor can any kind of political accommodation be reached through the redress of grievances, because the enemy's hostility is "limitless".

The Kean Commission's idea of conducting an investigation seems to be to dedicate its sixty staff to the validation of the official narrative. They rely on material that could never pass as evidence in a court of law. They completely drop any mention of the word "alleged" before the names of their hijackers. They identify their suspects as the suicide pilots with scant evidence, and fail to investigate mainstream media reports that found several alleged hijackers alive and well. They make no attempt at all to check whether the take-off planes were the same as the crashing ones.

The Kean Commission fails to explain how warnings were ignored, why FBI probes were blocked, why visas were issued illegally on laughably inadequate applications, how hijackers took control of the planes, why none of the eight pilots gave a hijacking alarm, why no aircraft debris was identified, how unspecified "phone calls" were made from the planes. It omits any mention of the negotiations with the Taliban in summer 2001 (when the US was already threatening war), fails to explain why each and every operative from an allegedly sophisticated terrorist organization such as Al-Qaeda, was traveling under their own name, and why, once they had got in, the alleged hijackers risked multiple flights out of the US and back.

The FBI's most-wanted poster for Osama Bin Laden does not cite the 9/11 crimes.

Credit: FBI website

Donald Rumsfeld, emissary of Pres. Ronald Reagan, shook hands with Saddam Hussein when the dictator was a U.S. ally against Iran.

Credit: Source unknown

The Commission made it a principle not to blame individuals for the "failings" exposed by the 9/11 events. The report is suffused with sympathy for the Federal Aviation Administration (FAA) and the North American Aerospace Defense Command (NORAD). There is no attempt to ask why they never thought anyone would pile an airliner into a US building, although missiles had been ranged around a G8 summit only months earlier to prevent just such an occurrence.

If it ever occurred to them that the government's plan to deal with the recognized threat from Al-Qaeda might simply have been to let the next attack happen and then invade Afghanistan, the Commission keeps it very quiet.

Despite the forest of footnotes, on the question of exactly what happened, the Kean Commission relies almost entirely on three sources only, all of which a reader without top security clearance has to take on trust: reports from the FBI's PENTTBOM Inquiry, Pentagon radar reconstructions of the hijacked plane's movements, and the transcripts of interviews with alleged terrorist masterminds, now captured.

There is little accounting in the report as to whether these sources were tested against phone records, samples of DNA from the alleged hijackers, plane debris, or any other independent sources. The devastating memo from FBI agent Colleen Rowley, alleging that her pre-9/11 inquiries were deliberately blocked, a major factor in the setting up of the Commission, is all but ignored.

The Kean Commission probed one or two topics that had to be answered: mainly, why NORAD failed to scramble fighters. But here they exonerate NORAD only to condemn the FAA and leaves the mystery untouched as to why pilots failed to signal they were being hijacked.

For 9/11 researchers, not to mention the skeptics, the most glaring feature of the Kean Commission is that despite its claim of full access to government documents, the report contains barely anything that had not already been forced into the open through leaks. This, they say, is a strong indication that the Commission was not an inquiry but a whitewash. One witness, whistleblower Sibel Edmonds, has stated that she spent hours giving the Commission vital evidence. Her reward was a gag order from the Department of Justice and silence in the Kean Report.

Kean did, however, personally break out of the straitjacket in an outburst in December 2003 when he said the attacks were "not something that had to happen" and officials had "simply failed". He later qualified these remarks under intense public pressure from other commissioners, and possibly even more pressure privately from the White House.

The Kean Commission also discovered that most of the Taliban regime had indeed opposed Al-Qaeda's 9/11 events as they said at the time.[16] The alternative to war in Afghanistan – fixing America's flawed defenses at home, while getting Osama bin Laden extradited – was ridiculed at the time in Washington and London: but three years later bin Laden was still on the run and Afghanistan and Iraq were still in flames. But for Cheney and the neocons – as Napoleon is said to have observed – it is not necessary that the truth be suppressed, only that it be delayed.[17]

Mullah Omar's offer to extradite bin Laden may have been genuine. It would have avoided war and bin Laden would have been in custody.

2:
Alternative
Scenarios

Official investigations have been stymied by secrecy, cronyism, and a refusal – even built into their terms of reference – to think the unthinkable. Much the same is true of the mainstream media. But – while not challenging the official story openly – they have reported facts that undermine it, like a mention at the end of a *Time* magazine report that senior Pentagon generals had cancelled flights the day before the 9/11 attacks. There have even been one or two major probes, like the *Wall Street Journal* investigation into the links between Al-Qaeda and Pakistan's ISI spy agency, which ended when journalist Daniel Pearl was kidnapped and murdered in Pakistan.

Book publishers and websites have provided the main forum for 9/11 skeptics fed by this stream of reports from the world's news media, downplayed by editors because they do not fit the official story. Independent researcher Paul Thompson has compiled a massively detailed 9/11 timeline of press reports starting in the early 1990s on the web and in 2004 published in book form.

Within weeks of the attacks, Nafeez Ahmed, a one-time Oxfam researcher, wrote *The War on Freedom*, suggesting that the attacks were allowed to happen to benefit the interests of key

Further, the process of transformation, even if it brings revolutionary change, is likely to be a long one, absent some catastrophic and catalyzing event – like a new Pearl Harbor. Domestic politics and industrial policy will shape the pace and

This prophetic quote is from *Rebuilding America's Defences* published in September 2000 by a neocon think-tank, The Project for a New American Century. PNAC was funded by Enron, backers of Bush and supporters of Tony Blair. The plan was to extend US military power to ensure there should be no competitors on the global stage.

figures in the US Government. This was a key source for Gore Vidal's seminal September 2002 article in the *Observer* (London) entitled: "The Enemy Within". On the "physical" side, engineer Eric Hufschmid has collated photographic evidence from the day of the attacks while A.K. Dewdney, a Canadian academic and one-time columnist for *Scientific American*, has concluded that most mobile phone calls from the hijacked planes would have been impossible. Best-selling French writer Thierry Meyssan sees the 9/11 attacks as a coup d'état from within the US military-industrial complex while German politician Andreas von Buelow, an intelligence specialist, has suggested that they were a false-flag operation by the CIA.[1]

Early in 2003 US theology professor David Ray Griffin published *The New Pearl Harbor*,[2] which rose through the best-seller lists while being ignored by the corporate media. The title was a reference to the original Japanese attack on Pearl Harbor that took America into the Second World War and was revisited by the Hollywood film *Pearl Harbor*, released only months before 9/11.

But Griffin's book title contained a more sinister reference too. In 2000 the Project for a New American Century – a think-tank run by the people who would later be known as the neocons around Bush – published a plan for a vastly expanded US military presence around the world.[3] The authors believed "The process of [military] transformation, even if it brings revolutionary change, is likely to be a long one, absent some catastrophic and catalyzing event – like a new Pearl Harbor."

As in the case of 9/11, there have been many allegations that the original Pearl Harbor attack was deliberately allowed to happen, enabling President Roosevelt to renege on his election promise not to enter the war. In a recent book, *Day of Deceit: The Truth about FDR and Pearl Harbor*, author Robert B. Stinnett, who believes the subterfuge was morally justified, presents a mass of Freedom of Information Act releases to show that Japanese codes were broken and information on the imminent attack was deliberately withheld from US forces on the ground. Stinnett details "about thirty-five people there in the book [including the President] that most certainly knew about it. And it's probably more than that."[4]

Sixty years after the events the Clinton administration refused Stinnett access to more files. Skeptics see an explanation for this extraordinary secrecy: allowing attacks to take place is an essential tactic of US Governments who wish to trick the public into war. Two other incidents are cited as evidence of this. The alleged Spanish sinking of the USS *Maine*, near Cuba, led to war against Spain in 1889 and the Gulf of Tonkin Incident in the summer of 1964 led to Congressional approval of the Vietnam War, though later, Congress was to conclude that this attack by the North Vietnamese had probably never occurred.[5]

Would They Do It?

There have been well-founded allegations of US agencies committing or colluding with multiple murders abroad, from the US press reports on the Phoenix assassination programme run by the CIA in Vietnam, which killed tens of thousands of communist suspects, to the thousands of deaths officially admitted by the Clinton White House under US-backed Governments in Guatemala in the 1980s.[6]

However, the claim is made in favour of the official 9/11 story that the US Government could not conceivably be a party to such an outrage as murdering their *own* people, though many accept the US Government has been involved in atrocities abroad. Nine/Eleven believers on the left say officials, though morally capable of such an act, would not want to take the risk of detection. Those on the right who even admit the possibility of such acts say they took place in the past, and were an unfortunate side-effect of the war against communism.

Some commentators who have examined the history of the neocons agree that the people around Bush are not traditional American conservatives at all, committed to small government, balanced budgets, and avoiding foreign entanglements. They are more like their ally Tony Blair, who has described himself as "third way" and "radical center". Others might describe them as ruthless pragmatists and part of a supranational network that would make little moral (as opposed to practical) distinction between killing Americans or Iraqis.[7]

Two central tenets of the "war on terror" could even be used as justification for allowing the 9/11 events, at least for hardliners in the security apparatus. First, the war was already underway in 2001 but the American people were lulled into a false sense of security, so at least the 9/11 events woke them up. Second, another attack might be much worse: in Cheney's words "we might lose tens or even hundreds of thousands of lives."[8]

Provoking terrorist attacks became official US Government policy in the summer of 2002 when the Pentagon's Defense Science Board proposed a $100 million team called the Proactive Pre-emptive Operations Group, or P2OG. This combination of special forces and intelligence agents will have "an entirely new capability to proactively, pre-emptively provoke responses from adversary/terrorist groups", according to the DSB's partially declassified report.

After being provoked, the action would be prevented and the perpetrators killed, but skeptics feel this proviso was put in for appearances and could easily be dropped. Whether P2OG was subsequently set up, or whether it already existed and the report merely proposed extending and financing its operations, is not known.[9]

Nine/Eleven Believers on the Left

If many mainstream citizens need persuading of the possibility that people within the US Government might be a party to mass murder, on the left and in the peace movement the arguments of 9/11 believers are quite different. Since the 9/11 events, the US has invaded Afghanistan and launched a fraudulent and illegal war in Iraq, they say. This amounts to mass murder on a far greater scale than 9/11. Why make allegations that might not even be true? To 9/11 skeptics this is a disastrous political miscalculation – a population terrorized by the 9/11 attacks is unlikely to show much concern for the foreign victims of a war they think has been started by a highly potent enemy.

When we spoke off the record to a senior US journalist, a vehement opponent of Bush, he was reluctant to doubt the official 9/11 story: "never underestimate the incompetence of the Pentagon" was his observation. In his view, there probably was a 9/11 cover-up but only to hide incompetence in allowing the attacks to happen. Since the Kean Commission report was published, incompetence has been more or less incorporated into the official story, although it was unmentionable in the months after 9/11.

A third argument is put forward by some academics on the US left: the "conspiracism" theory. This holds that suspicions about government are due to ignorance and feelings of helplessness. Blaming plotters is a political blind alley, comparable to the Nazi tactic of blaming the ills of capitalism on a "Jewish conspiracy". However, most 9/11 skeptics hardly fit the picture of the uneducated poor seen as prey to conspiracy theories.[10]

Nine/Eleven believers also accuse skeptics of flawed methodology, gobbling up large numbers of strange coincidences and apparent inconsistencies in the official story and jumping to conclusions. Skeptics respond that it is a matter of judgment how many coincidences amount to a prima facie case, and that the US Government is, on its record, not an innocent bystander but a chief suspect.

It is true that 9/11 skeptics often fail to distinguish between suspicious coincidences and proof. But they argue that too many suspicious circumstances do amount to proof so long as they are not selected unfairly. In this case they seem to blight not the periphery but the heart of the official 9/11 story: the identity and modus operandi of the alleged hijackers, FBI activity before 9/11, the physical evidence at the crime scenes, and the subsequent investigations.

Nine/Eleven believers of all persuasions are on stronger ground on another issue: that of secrecy. The FBI's general policy of withholding evidence in any criminal investigation – so as to avoid giving help to conspirators who may be still at large – is often taken by the many skeptics in the US who are libertarians as evidence in itself for a cover-up.

How Would a 9/11 Plot Work?

For supporters of the official story it is a central belief that a 9/11 plot could not have been kept secret, because it would have involved too many people. Is this correct? Here is how a plot might be structured . . .

1. Key senior officials in the know, the A Team, create smokescreens, paralyze government departments before the attacks, oversee a cover-up afterwards and supervise any X Team.

2. Other officials, media editors and journalists, the B Team, aid in the paralysis, help with the cover-up, often unwittingly. They are given different stories depending on their role. They might be told, for instance, that an intelligence operation has gone embarrassingly wrong or that any deviation from the official account might provide terrorists with useful information.

3. If there is a proactive plan, a small team of operatives, the X Team, carry it out.

The less active the plot, the more it could be accomplished by middle-ranking rather than top officials. For instance, a decision to let a genuine Al-Qaeda attack go ahead could be made by the leader of the team monitoring the hijackers. However, 9/11 skeptics mostly support the view that authorization came from the top, citing the failure of any official at any level to be disciplined for the apparent incompetence that even Thomas Kean denounced.

X Team operatives might come from the Pentagon's Delta Force or be recruited from the CIA's Clandestine Service (CS). This is what Congress stated of the CS in 1996: "The Clandestine Service is the only part of the IC (Intelligence Community), indeed of the government, where hundreds of employees on a daily basis are directed to break extremely serious laws in countries around the world."[11]

Oliver North's Iran-Contra operation involved clandestine air flights, multiple illegal arms shipments between three continents and hot money transfers, yet it was years before it was exposed. With the more spectacular 9/11 operation, believers say that as the plot gets bolder, the risk of detection or leakage would go up.

On the other hand, skeptics say the massive psychological impact of the attacks, the declaration of war and the support of Washington and Europe for the "war on terror" made it far harder to question the official line.

How easy would it be to paralyze the government in step two? Pretty easy, according to the findings of the Kean Commission, who detail the very real paralysis of the FBI before the attacks, and of the Federal Aviation Administration (FAA) during them. The Kean Commission assumed this paralysis was accidental.

Because of the "need to know" principle essential to all intelligence work, even senior officials involved in the paralysis would not need to be told what they were covering up. For instance, senior FBI officials might be told there was already a (fictitious) operation in place to deal with the suspected hijackers, and to preserve it they must stop their agents from interfering.

Paralysis of official investigative machinery was, as we have seen, carried out very effectively by Cheney after the attacks. Many 9/11 skeptics have speculated that there was an incriminating "stand down" order in NORAD that stopped planes scrambling in time. Instead, what has emerged is a change of standing orders made in June 2001, making it much more likely that intercepts would be delayed by creating a long chain of decision making. Paralysis can be carried out silently and effectively without an incriminating paper trail. It can be excused on the concept that appears again and again in the official story: misjudgment and incompetence.

For the sort of incriminating leak that 9/11 believers would predict, an A Team or X Team operative must blow the whistle, evade reprisals, and be believed. Otherwise, B Team officials can only give their essentially negative indirect evidence that something is being covered up – hardly a surprise in any modern government, let alone in Washington. One of the most suspicious aspects of the 9/11 story is that a series of officials have indeed come forward with evidence that suggests an intentional paralysis of the US Government.

The policing of X Team operatives, destruction of evidence, and nobbling of expert witnesses that could blow the plot apart is carried out by a small covert team, an adjunct to the X Team. The signs of this operation would be threats, retracted evidence, and disappearances of witnesses. This has indeed happened. The more general cover-up is organized by the A Team. By now they have much more power over the B Team – war has been declared, the story has been bought by the media, and people disputing it are "conspiracy theorists".

An official investigation is little threat, so long as the only hypothesis is the official story. As the Kean Commission shows, the more evidence dredged up, the easier it is to disregard the awkward bits.

Many 9/11 skeptics see the attacks, essentially, as a psychological warfare operation – against the American public. The World Trade Center is a symbol of US power whose destruction needs to be avenged. It is also a symbol of global integration, so the attack serves indirectly to discredit the "anti-globalization" world justice movement. The Pentagon is chosen to underline the notion that the US is now at war.

Friendly foreign governments are ready and willing to declare a "war on terror". They calculate that the attacks will force Washington to engage with the world, undermining both "isolationists" in the US and the global justice movement. They also offer the obvious benefits of easier repression of their own dissident movements.

The plot works, not because the plotters have carefully tied up every loose end, but because no piece of evidence is compelling enough for anyone in the corporate media to stake their careers on. Like any good con trick, it also works because the victims want to believe it.

The fact that so little of the conflicting evidence has been properly investigated by the corporate media and the Kean Commission is in itself the most powerful argument that plotters in the US Government would be right not to fear detection. Another indication a plot could go undetected comes from the US military itself, as we shall see . . .

Operation Northwoods

The Pentagon plan that might have served as an early draft of a US Government plot on 9/11 is available on the public record. Operation Northwoods, released to author James Bamford from the archives under Freedom of Information laws, showed that the Joint Chiefs of Staff drew up and approved detailed agent provocateur plans. "We could develop a Communist Cuban terror campaign in the Miami area . . . and even in Washington . . . we could sink a boatload of Cubans en route to Florida (real or simulated)."

Here are the details of a 9/11-type plan officially proposed by the US Joint Chiefs of Staff as part of Operation Northwoods. The plan involved creating a decoy charter flight of holidaymakers bound for a destination that would take its flight path over Cuba. An aircraft at Elgin Air Force base would be painted and numbered as an exact duplicate for a civil-registered aircraft owned by the CIA. The duplicate would become the official flight and take on the specially selected passengers, "all boarded under carefully prepared aliases". The actual registered aircraft would be converted to a drone (a remote-controlled unmanned aircraft). The planes would cross in the air south of Florida to create an apparently continuous radar track.

Then the passenger-carrying double would disappear, descending to minimum altitude and going directly into an auxiliary field at Elgin. There the "passengers" would be taken away to resume their normal identities, perhaps as military personnel, and the aircraft

TOP SECRET SPECIAL HANDLING NOFORN

THE JOINT CHIEFS OF STAFF
WASHINGTON 25, D.C.

UNCLASSIFIED

13 March 1962

MEMORANDUM FOR THE SECRETARY OF DEFENSE

Subject: Justification for US Military Intervention
in Cuba (TS)

1. The Joint Chiefs of Staff have considered the attached
Memorandum for the Chief of Operations, Cuba Project, which
responds to a request of that office for brief but precise
description of pretexts which would provide justification
for US military intervention in Cuba.

2. The Joint Chiefs of Staff recommend that the
proposed memorandum be forwarded as a preliminary submission
suitable for planning purposes. It is assumed that there
will be similar submissions from other agencies and that
these inputs will be used as a basis for developing a
time-phased plan. Individual projects can then be
considered on a case-by-case basis.

3. Further, it is assumed that a single agency will be
given the primary responsibility for developing military
and para-military aspects of the basic plan. It is
recommended that this responsibility for both overt and
covert military operations be assigned the Joint Chiefs of
Staff.

For the Joint Chiefs of Staff:

L. L. LEMNITZER
Chairman
Joint Chiefs of Staff

SYSTEMATICALLY REVIEWED
BY JCS ON _____
CLASSIFICATION CONTINUED

1 Enclosure
Memo for Chief of Operations, Cuba Project   EXCLUDED FROM GDS

EXCLUDED FROM AUTOMATIC
REGRADING; DOD DIR 5200.10
DOES NOT APPLY

TOP SECRET SPECIAL HANDLING NOFORN

The 9/11 events could have been an update of a Pentagon plan from the 1960s. The Joint Chiefs
headed their letter: "Subject – Justification for U.S. military intervention in Cuba".

Credit: U.S. Department of Defense

switched back to its original status. The drone aircraft meanwhile would continue to fly the filed flight plan. Over Cuba, the drone would be transmitting on the international distress frequency a Mayday message stating he was under attack by Cuban MiG aircraft. The transmission would be interrupted by destruction of the aircraft, which would be triggered by radio signal. This would allow International Civil Aviation Organization (ICAO) radio stations in the western hemisphere to tell the US authorities what had happened to the aircraft, instead of the report originating from the US. (We are grateful to James Bamford for sections of his synopsis of the Pentagon plan, *Body of Secrets: Anatomy of the Ultra-Secret National Security Agency*, 2001.)

The Northwoods plan as presented to the President did not explicitly propose killing US citizens – this would have been a criminal offense. However, there could have been authorized or unauthorized add-ons. Some 9/11 skeptics see the collapse of the towers or the anthrax attacks as add-ons to the basic plot. Perhaps fearing some sort of unauthorized add-on, Robert Kennedy, the US Attorney General, vetoed Northwoods.

The Northwoods plan shows that at the top level of government people were capable of conceiving something so complicated, devious, and fraudulent. Worse still, it shows they calculated that the logistics of the plot would be feasible and a cover-up achievable.

Behind the Looking-Glass

For more radical 9/11 skeptics, Operation Northwoods explains the events of 9/11 neatly enough: the events were essentially a hoax – or as some Middle Eastern observers have it, a conjuring trick. Either planes were swapped or remote-controlled takeovers of the supposed hijacked planes were achieved, using a small X Team to run the attacks and steal the identities of the fictitious hijackers.

However, at least in public, most mainstream 9/11 skeptics argue for a far less active role for US-based plotters: permitting or aiding genuine hijackers who are working for Al-Qaeda (or at least believe they are). They do not have an Operation Northwoods-type blueprint as evidence, but they cite the very nature of the intelligence world as their model.

In autumn 2004 the BBC ran a series of programmes analysing Al-Qaeda, *The Power of Nightmares* by Adam Curtis, arguing it had been blown up out of all proportion by Western propagandists looking for an enemy. This, three years too late, was what most 9/11 skeptics had been saying all along. Al-Qaeda has often been an ally, as well as an enemy, of the US. In contrast to the simplistic good and evil world of the corporate media, the reality is of a vast gray area of confusion, double agents, and mixed loyalties.

Phillip Agee resigned in the 1970s from the CIA, Victor Ostrovsky left Israel's Mossad in the late 1980s, and Howard Marks retired from high-level drug dealing in the 1990s. Each has written revealingly about the worlds they left, and the picture they each paint is the one described by FBI whistleblower Sibel Edmonds in 2004.[12] A translator at FBI HQ Sibel Edmonds was sacked in March 2002 after she said she had seen evidence of "treason" while working at FBI HQ. She has explained: "I can tell you that the issue, on one side, boils down to money – a lot of money. And it boils down to people and their connections with this money . . . The most significant information that we were receiving came from counter-intelligence, and certain criminal investigations, and issues that have to do with money laundering operations . . . I keep underlining semi-legit organizations and following the money. When you do that the picture gets grim. It gets really ugly . . . And you start trying to go to the root of it and it's getting into somebody's political campaign, and somebody's lobbying. And people don't want to be traced back to this money."

Enemies and friends, especially since the days of the Cold War ended, are often interchangeable, alliances are always ad hoc and driven as much by money and power as by credo. Al-Qaeda seems to have been allied with the West as recently as the bombing of Kosovo in 1999.

Why destroy an organization if you can have it working for you for free? If you can infiltrate it you can limit its operations and keep a finger on eager new recruits. If you destroy it, it will only be replaced by a new organization that will have to be infiltrated all over again. However, terrorist or criminal organizations do not have personnel along for the ride. Your agents inside the organization will need to maintain their cover by helping it, so you will inevitably be helping the enemy indirectly.

The best strategy for survival as a high-level terrorist or drug dealer is to be a double agent offering value to both sides. This is particularly easy to get away with in the anarchic world of Islamic fundamentalism, where Al-Qaeda is more of a network than an army.

Many intelligence agencies have sections that are licensed to break the law. In the case of the CIA's Clandestine Service, we have seen that this licence is official, at least for activities abroad. A senior "bad apple" in an intelligence service, with people under his command and agents in "enemy" organizations, has huge scope for wrongdoing. The "need to know" culture of secrecy can ensure that an unauthorized operation is kept secret from officials or even supervisors who might object. Corrupt police caught with drugs, for instance, can claim they were conducting a sting operation.

The scope for illegal operations is even greater with the backing of officials at the very top. If you aid or allow an organization like Al-Qaeda to carry out an operation, you can always say you were running an infiltration or sting operation that went wrong. However, as US President Franklin D. Roosevelt is supposed to have said: "In politics nothing happens by accident, if it happens you can bet it was planned that way."

LIHOP: Letting It Happen On Purpose

In the early days after the 9/11 events knowledge of Operation Northwoods was minimal. Memories of Vietnam and the Phoenix programme had faded even among older activists and were mere history for a new generation. Even for many 9/11 skeptics, it seemed unthinkable that the CIA could engineer the attacks or actively help the hijackers succeed. And so, the let-it-happen-on-purpose or LIHOP theory was born. This scenario seems to fit in with the way politicians normally operate – allowing things to happen, while shifting responsibility elsewhere.

LIHOP holds that in 2000 Washington is keen to get a military presence in the Middle East oilfields and desperate to do something about Al-Qaeda. Unable to convince the US public to go to war, senior officials consciously decide to ignore evidence of the impending attack, intending that it should succeed.

The allegation from White House anti-terrorism coordinator Richard Clarke, that officials decided to downplay the Al-Qaeda threat because they were simply not persuaded it was a priority, would be a spectacular misjudgment, but it would not be a crime. We would describe this scenario as within the official story. LIHOP starts when officials get evidence of a plot and consciously choose to ignore it with the aim of allowing it to happen.

We described the ingredients for a 9/11 plot, with an A Team of senior officials paralyzing the government's defenses, and an X Team of active covert operatives. In LIHOP there is no X Team. Supporters say it complies with the scientific rule known as Occam's Razor: that the simpler theory is always preferable. Evidence of LIHOP can normally be excused as incompetence and involves much less risk to plotters on the A Team. A LIHOP plot would dovetail with the views of cynics like our

Washington journalist who find almost any level of apparent incompetence credible.

Here are two LIHOP scenarios:

- The A Team are the now notorious top neocon officials. They receive information there is an attack coming. Perhaps they underestimate the attackers' ambitions, perhaps they convince themselves America needs to be woken up. They decide to allow the attack to happen and do their best to paralyze the FBI and confuse the FAA and NORAD with involved administrative measures and new procedures. The neocons and Al-Qaeda are both, in their own way, set on war and both get lucky.

- Since the Soviet pull-out from Afghanistan, the CIA has maintained some contacts with Al-Qaeda. A well-placed operative is keeping the CIA informed of the plot and a top secret plan is worked out to foil the hijacks at the last moment in a dramatic way. Key FBI officials are told to block their own investigations because the CIA has the matter in hand. A general smokescreen is put over events, perhaps a military exercise is scheduled for the day of the attacks. An official from the A Team takes control of the CIA plan and wrecks it at the last minute, enabling the attacks to succeed.

MIHOP: Make It Happen On Purpose

Starting on the moral foundations, so to speak, of LIHOP, there is a wide range of scenarios involving positive actions to help the hijackers – or even create the attacks in a revamp of Operation Northwoods. Make-it-happen-on-purpose (MIHOP) proponents say the A Team would understand that, legally, there is little difference between LIHOP and a Northwoods-type hoax. They might calculate that, for a little extra risk to themselves, they could make sure of getting exactly what they want by taking a more interventionist role.

MIHOP proponents argue that the A Team would never take the risk of pure LIHOP, leaving several teams of genuine suicide hijackers free to do what they liked with their flying bombs. Supposing they hit a nuclear power station, the Capitol, or the side of the Pentagon where Rumsfeld was sitting that morning?

Besides the Operation Northwoods school, which holds there were no genuine hijackers, MIHOP scenarios propose the planting of agents into Al-Qaeda to help organize the plot, taking over hijacked aircraft by remote control or simply aiding and abetting Al-Qaeda by systematically clearing a path for the hijackers. They often cite physical evidence (which we examine) seemingly showing that the official story is false in a fundamental way.

Ironically, a MIHOP-type scenario was at the heart of the White House narrative for over two years, with the mantra from the neocons that an attack like this could not have been carried out without the help of an intelligence service: in their judgment, Iraq. Their high point came with the anthrax attacks, which were initially blamed on Iraq. Here are some MIHOP scenarios:

- There is a consensus at the top of the US Government that with the next Al-Qaeda attack Afghanistan will be invaded. Meanwhile, the 9/11 hijackers have been penetrated and officials decide to bring the scheme to fruition with active help. Perhaps they give a tip-off that multiple Pentagon exercises are planned for the day – perhaps one of the organizers is a CIA asset.

- Officials might maintain control by tailing the hijacked aircraft discreetly with unmarked fighters ready to shoot them down if they go off course, by rigging the aircraft with remote-controlled overrides, or just by tampering with the flight computers.

■ Republican lawyer Stanley Hilton, a biographer and one time senior aide to 1996 Presidential candidate Bob Dole has tried to bring a lawsuit on behalf of many 9/11 victims. He told dissident radio presenter Alex Jones: "I went to school with some of these neocons. At the University of Chicago, in the late 60s with Wolfowitz and and Feith and several of the others and so I know these people personally. And we used to talk about this stuff all of the time . . . how to turn the US into a presidential dictatorship by manufacturing a bogus Pearl Harbor event . . . The hijackers we retained . . . They were double agents, paid by the FBI and the CIA to spy on Arab groups in this country. They were controlled . . . nerve gas kills everybody on board the plane . . ."[13]

■ Even farther down the spectrum of complicity are scenarios for an updated Operation Northwoods. Perhaps bogus passengers and drone aircraft are used, as in the Northwoods plan, or remote control is used to take over genuine aircraft. No suicide hijackers exist. The people named as the hijackers have had their identities stolen. Along with the rest of the people who apparently boarded the planes, they are either dead or living under different identities, as the Pentagon planned in the Northwoods project.

Any basic MIHOP or LIHOP scenario can have add-ons, where officials in the know create extra twists to the plot, either authorized or not. It may have been because of the risk of unauthorized add-ons that the Kennedy White House vetoed the Northwoods plan. Here are the main ones that have been discussed:

■ There is now a wide agreement the anthrax attacks were some sort of add-on to the 9/11 events. They are, of course, presumed by the ever-optimistic Washington media to be an unauthorized add-on by rogue operators in the bio weapons industry.

■ The Twin Towers are pre-rigged with explosives. If this comes to light it can be explained as a safety measure to bring them straight down, avoiding a truly disastrous sideways fall. The plan is coordinated from the conveniently placed and totally secure command center already installed in WTC 7.

■ The Pentagon attack. Even if there are genuine hijackers, allowing them to fly into Washington is too risky. A drone Boeing 757 is used or a smaller, more manageable plane, painted in American Airlines colors.

Research into MIHOP issues focuses mainly on the physical evidence at the crash sites and the identities of the hijackers. Surprisingly, as we shall see, there is in fact a considerable body of evidence to support MIHOP scenarios and the various add-ons. Many 9/11 skeptics agree there were two groups of hijackers and point to evidence that the supposed organizers from the "Hamburg cell" are simply not credible as suicidal fundamentalists.

Other Scenarios

We have now seen four general approaches to the 9/11 mystery: the official story, the incompetence theory, LIHOP and MIHOP. In the following pages we examine some other theories.

Cheney and Bush have repeatedly suggested that Al-Qaeda was helped by Iraq. The anthrax attacks, initially blamed on Iraq, gave a powerful boost to this view. As it became clear the anthrax came from a domestic source the neocons claimed that leading hijacker Mohammed Atta had met with an Iraqi agent in Prague Airport. However, the Prague Airport story collapsed when the FBI placed Atta somewhere else that day and the Czech security chief repudiated the identification of Atta. The Kean Commission gave the Iraq connection short shrift.

The second suspect for the role of complicit foreign intelligence service was Saudi Arabia. The majority of the hijackers had Saudi passports, bin Laden was a Saudi, Saudi Arabia was the home of Islamic fundamentalism, there were rumors that Al-Qaeda had widespread support in Saudi Arabia: on a quick reading it all made sense.

The view that Saudi Arabia was somehow responsible for 9/11 was indirectly promoted by the film maker Michael Moore in *Fahrenheit 9/11*. In the film, Moore plays video footage of Bush in the Florida schoolroom as he hears the news of the second hit on the morning of 9/11. Moore emphasizes Bush's peculiar furtive expression as he hears the message whispered in his ear by chief of staff Andrew Card. The official story holds that the message was: "America is under attack".

Moore suggests that this is the moment Bush realizes that his Saudi friends have somehow betrayed him. Moore's view is based on the evident ties between the Bush dynasty and the Saudi oil business: because the Bush family was linked so closely to the Saudi elite, a no-go area was created in the US defenses, enabling Al-Qaeda to strike.

Washington journalist Gerald Posner's *Why America Slept*[14] took the allegations much farther. Posner apparently received a fascinating leak from US intelligence sources. They were able to trick captive Abu Zubaydah, an alleged Al-Qaeda leader, into believing he had been moved to Saudi Arabia. With the aid of truth drugs, and believing he was talking to sympathetic Saudi intelligence personnel, Zubaydah offered the information that five key top officials in Saudi and Pakistan were allies of Al-Qaeda. To confirm the story Zubaydah was able to provide their phone numbers.

Four of the officials died under unusual circumstances in the months after this, says Posner. The fifth, Prince Turki Al-faisal bin Abdul Aziz was Saudi intelligence chief on 9/11 and then became Ambassador to London. There is no evidence of Prince Turki having any connection with Al-Qaeda. He has said "I have had no contacts with bin Laden since 1990, and have never had any contacts with Al-Qaeda".

The main Al-Qaeda contact in Saudi, Posner suggests, was Prince Ahmed bin Salman bin Abdul Aziz, described as a publisher and racehorse enthusiast who won the Kentucky Derby in 2002.

However, it is implausible that the highest strata of the Saudi royal family would be working for Al-Qaeda, an organization that is dedicated to their overthrow. Moreover, with Washington's powerful pro-Israel lobby gunning for it, it seems odd that anyone from the Saudi elite would conduct a hostile operation against America using their own nationals and in the case of Zubaydah not even bothering with a cut out (or, a mutually trusted intermediary who handles communications between espionage agents).

If the four were indeed murdered, who carried out the murders? Al-Qaeda hardly seems to have the capacity to carry off a series of targeted car crashes, a heart attack and a plane crash. How could Saudi influence explain the apparent paralysis of US military defenses? For skeptics Posner's evidence can be read very differently: Abu Zubaydah betrayed Al-Qaeda's true chain of command, which ran through the pro Western Saudi and Pakistani intelligence services to the CIA and perhaps MI6 in London.

One virtue of the Saudi theory is that it explains the paralysis of the FBI: the aggressive obstruction from HQ experienced by several FBI field offices when they tried to investigate flight schools and potential hijackers in summer of 2001. As well as the evidence we cite later, French writers Jean-Charles Brisard and Guillaume Dasquie say in their book *Forbidden Truth* that the FBI was blocked, to protect the Saudi Royal family and the interests in Afghanistan of Enron, the energy corporation which backed Bush and Blair financially and went spectacularly bankrupt in autumn 2001.

The key source for *Forbidden Truth* was John O'Neill, until summer 2001 the FBI's most experienced counter-terrorism agent (see illustration), who resigned in protest. Moreover there is little doubt that the White House was negotiating with the Taliban with a view to getting approval for the Unocal/Enron pipeline through Afghanistan and the extradition of bin Laden (reportedly threatening "a carpet of gold or a carpet of bombs").[15]

But as it stands the theory that the White House put a block on the FBI to protect the private interests of the Saudis or Enron has a serious flaw. Why would a block on Al-Qaeda investigations in the US make the Taliban want to approve the oil deal or extradite bin Laden? How would it protect the Saudi royal family? Giving Al-Qaeda a free hand in the US could only lead to the sort of disaster that occurred on 9/11, a disaster that friendly intelligence agencies were warning of strenuously at the time O'Neill resigned.

John O'Neill was a senior FBI agent working for years on Al-Qaeda. "He was the paramount, most knowledgeable agent we had in the FBI, probably in the government, with respect to counter-intelligence matters," says then FBI Director Louis Freeh. In August 2001, angry at the White House – ordered block on investigations, he resigned. He was offered a job at the World Trade Center by its new owners and died in the 9/11 attacks.[16]

The best course to protect top Saudis from embarrassment and strengthen the US negotiating hand with the Taliban would be obvious to political operators with far less cunning than Dick Cheney and Karl Rove: instruct the FBI to arrest and quietly deport all Al-Qaeda suspects before they made the news. The Enron block, say skeptics, is real enough, but rather than incompetent bungling by the White House it is a "limited hangout" (CIA cover story) for the deliberate paralysis of America's defenses by the A Team.

The Events

3: Flight 11: No Mayday Calls

Several questions asked by 9/11 skeptics arise again and again. How were the hijackers able to board the planes with weapons? How were they able to take over the planes? Why were no hijack warnings given and why did air traffic controllers fail to report suspected hijackings to the military in breach of standard procedures? We offer an overview of these issues, then we look at each flight separately.

US airport security was tightened up considerably after an explosion aboard TWA Flight 800 in November 1996 and the Gore Commission recommendations that followed. Besides the universally used X-ray machines and metal-detector walkthrough arches, airports introduced

Box cutters and meal-tray plastic knives were supposedly used to take control of the four airliners.

The airports involved in 9/11 all had X-ray machines for viewing carry-on luggage. According to the official 9/11 narrative this system failed in three separate airports.

Copyright: L-3 Communications

the automatic requirement of photo ID, as well as "sniffer" dogs on security teams. Checkpoints uncovered about 24 million prohibited items a year (TSA website, author's projection).[1]

One early explanation for the takeover of the planes was that the hijackers had managed to access the secure areas. Undercover government inspections revealed a possible loophole, as a Mr Mead of the FAA told the Kean Commission: "During the late 1990s we successfully accessed secure areas in 68 per cent of our tests . . . once we entered the secure areas we were able to walk on the plane unchallenged 117 times." But this would have been no use to hijackers in First Class, who would have required seat numbers conforming to the cabin crew's seating plan.

On 15 May 2002, the President's press officer, Ari Fleischer, stated: "the people who committed the 9/11 events used box cutters and plastic knives to get around America's system of protecting against hijackings." But while several of the controversial mobile phone calls referred to stabbings, there is very little evidence of the use of box cutters and none of plastic knives.

On Flight 11, attendant Betty Ong reported by in-flight phone: "we can't breathe in business class. Somebody's got mace or something." Would this mean that hijackers had smuggled anti-tear gas masks aboard, too? She was first reported to have told of a shooting, but that was later withdrawn as a communications error. She told of two flight attendants being stabbed but made no mention of box cutters nor of plastic knives (nor of passengers, oddly enough).

On Flight 175, businessman Peter Hanson called his father and said, "Oh, my God! They just stabbed the airline hostess. I think the airline is being hijacked." On Flight 93, a flight attendant said by mobile phone that a hijacker had a "bomb strapped on". Passenger Todd Beamer referred to a "terrorist with a bomb" in a mobile phone call. Another passenger, Tom Burnett, told his wife by mobile phone that he had heard that a pilot had been "knifed".

On Flight 77, Theodore Olson, US Solicitor General, told the *Daily Telegraph* six months after the attacks that his third wife, Barbara, had made two collect (reverse charges) in-flight phone calls to his office. The only weapons she is supposed to have mentioned were knives and "cardboard cutters". Without offering proper substantiation of the phone call involved, the US mass media amplified Ted Olson's reference to "cardboard cutters" into the hijackers' weapon of choice on all the stricken planes.[2]

If prohibited weapons had been smuggled aboard, the airlines could have faced ruinous lawsuits. If, however, it could penetrate the public mind that only legal box cutters and meal-tray plastic knives had been used, neither the airlines nor the FAA could be held legally responsible.

Transportation Secretary Mineta told the Commission: "The FAA regulation referred to blades of four inches or greater as prohibited items. And so a box cutter was really less than four inches. Now, on the other hand, the airline industry had a guideline. And in that guideline, they did prohibit box cutters, as it was in that guideline."

But the Kean Commission uncovered a different airline industry policy, one that specifically covered checkpoints and which flatly contradicted Mineta's testimony: "While FAA rules did not expressly prohibit knives with blades under four inches long, the airlines' checkpoint operations guide (which was developed in cooperation with the FAA), explicitly permitted them."[3]

The Kean Commission had little discussion of the vital question of how the hijackers could take over the planes without the pilots issuing a warning to ground control, but it was greatly exercised by how long the hijackers' presumed knives were. For 9/11 believers this is a case of American legalism, for skeptics it shows the Kean Commission was more interested in protecting vested interests than discovering the truth.

No Fighters Scrambled

As discussed earlier, the major part of any plot from within the US to allow the 9/11 events would be the paralysis of the US apparatus tasked with America's defenses. So it is not surprising that 9/11 skeptics have focused on the failure of NORAD to scramble jets in time to intercept any of the hijacked planes.

Whether or not they could or should have shot the jetliners down, NORAD's fighters should have intercepted them. But it is officially agreed that no fighter intercepted any of the rogue airliners between 8.14am, when Flight 11 went off air, and 10.03am when Flight 93 apparently crashed in Pennsylvania.

Standard procedures apply for the Federal Aviation Administration and the US military, namely the National Military Command Center (NMCC) located under the east side of the Pentagon, and the north-eastern air defense sector (NEADS) of

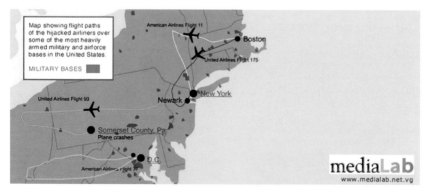

Medialab merged two maps, placing the approximate routes of the aircraft over the US Air Force bases beneath them (dotted lines should show where the planes were lost to official view). Under normal conditions, no rogue airplane goes anywhere near a US Air Force base without getting investigated. The Pentagon's PAVE PAWS system boasts on its website that it "does not miss anything occurring in North American airspace".

Copyright: Medialab

Radar operators at USAF bases along the rogue airliners' routes were capable of scanning hundreds of square miles of sky.

Copyright: USAF

the North American Aerospace Defense Command (NORAD). The procedures require the FAA to contact the NMCC when it suspects that an aircraft has been hijacked.

The official attitude to a hijacking is crystal clear: get planes scrambled as soon as possible. Officials must err on the side of caution and act on suspicion, not certainty. The signs to watch are: deviation from the flight plan; loss of transponder message; or loss of radio contact. The FAA must request assistance from the NMCC. In all cases, a possible hijacking must be treated as an actual hijacking, and the FAA will use "the most expeditious means" of notifying the high command.[4]

The NMCC, in its turn, will tell NORAD to activate or "scramble" jets from the nearest Air Force base (AFB) with jets on alert. Procedures for intercepting a rogue jet are by now well-known: the approaching fighter rocks its wingtips to attract the pilot's attention, or swings in front of the aircraft. It may fire tracer rounds in the path of the aircraft. The FAA says there were sixty-seven interceptions in the period September 2000 to June 2001. None of this occurred on 9/11. There have been three versions of what did happen.

Controllers at regional air route traffic control centers like this one played the main role in the events of 9/11, apparently "losing" all four hijacked aircraft for periods of up to thirty-five minutes, because someone had switched off, modified, or jammed the jetliners' transponder units. The "disappearances" provided an opportunity for black-ops, such as aerial rendezvous and plane substitutions. Copyright: NASA

General Myers, acting chairman of the Joint Chiefs of Staff, told the Senate Armed Services Committee on 13 September that "when it became clear what the threat was, we did scramble fighter aircraft . . . That order, to the best of my knowledge, was after the Pentagon was struck." (He overlooked standard procedure, which did not require threat identification for intercept.) Two days later, the NORAD spokesperson, Major Mike Snyder, told the media that the USAF scrambled no fighters until after the Pentagon was hit. The Pentagon was hit at 9.38am, which puts the USAF scramble order fifty-two minutes after the North Tower attack and no fewer than eighty-four minutes after Flight 11 first gave signs of being hijacked.

At this point, the government and the Pentagon were wide open to the charge of suspending standard procedures on 9/11. Yet on 18 September, a NORAD press release said planes had been scrambled but had arrived too late. The notification times of the FAA and the scramble order times implied it was all the FAA's fault.

In February 2005 the Commission made things even worse for the FAA and the White House with a delayed report recording that the FAA had mentioned in a spring 2001 circular to airports that "the intent of the hijacker [might be] not to exchange hostages for prisoners, but to commit suicide in a spectacular explosion". In the six months before 9/11 federal aviation officials had received 52 intelligence summaries, half the total, which mentioned Osama bin Laden and Al-Qaeda (*New York Times*, February 10, 2005).

Congressman Henry Waxman wrote angrily to Bush, suggesting the report released within 48 hours of Rice's confirmation as Secretary of State had been delayed to save embarrassment to Rice who said as late as 16 May 2002: "I don't think anybody could have predicted that these people would . . . try to use an airplane as a missile, a hijacked airplane as a missile."[5]

In the case of Flight 11, the first to be hijacked, NORAD said the FAA had not notified it until 8.40am, or twenty-six minutes after the signs of a hijacking. Nine/Eleven skeptics and believers alike have asked why no FAA personnel were dismissed or even publicly reprimanded for incompetence.

NORAD's revised version did not exonerate the Air Force, either. Its own timeline now showed it had taken four minutes to issue a scramble order. Moreover, the order had been issued to Otis AFB, which is in Massachusetts, over 150 miles away from New York, instead of to McGuire AFB, which lies much closer, in New Jersey. The jets had not taken off for another eight minutes, leaving at 8.52.

Even so, the F-15s which took off from Otis should have arrived over New York City airspace in time to intercept the second plane. They had been alerted about it at 8.43am, twenty minutes before the South Tower was hit. Going at full speed, they should have been over Manhattan by 9.00. At 9.02, however, the fighters were still seventy-one miles away, according to NORAD's second version of events.

The Kean Commission brought its sixty staff and $15 million to bear and came up with a third version. According to the Commission, FAA controllers spent a long time suspecting that Flight 11 had been hijacked before they became certain and took action. This, as mentioned above, violated procedure, whereby controllers must act on suspicion immediately. They then did not contact the NMCC directly but "started notifying their chain of command".

In sharp contrast with the protocol outlined above, getting a scramble order now involved numerous telephone calls taking anything up to half an hour. The FAA and NORAD were bogged down in hopeless bureaucracy, and no one was really in charge, explains the Commission. Then NORAD, acting on the wrong information from the FAA, confused Flight 175 with Flight 77, hence the failure to intercept Flight 77.

This raises the question of how the FAA ran the world's biggest air transport system. It had 44,039 employees, nearly 18,000 of them air traffic controllers skilled at reading radar screens. It had some 600 radar and communications towers. On 9/11 the FAA was juggling some 4,166 individual aircraft. It succeeded in grounding every single one of them in a very short time, yet it seemed unable to get anyone on the phone to NMCC in line with its statutory duties.

We will follow the Kean Commission's account from now on. Flight attendant Amy Sweeney is supposed to have informed American Airlines of Flight 11's hijacking at 8.21am. A mystery pilot (presumably a hijacker on Flight 11) says: "We have some planes" at 8.24, but according to the Kean Commission, the FAA does not understand its significance for nearly thirty minutes. But it was 8.43am before NORAD was informed of one or two probable hijackings. Three minutes later, at 8.46, an aircraft resembling Flight 11 hit the northern Twin Tower.

Alerts should have been circulating among all the FAA's regional air traffic centers of apparent coordinated hijackings in progress. Instead, when Flight 77 was hijacked three minutes later, FAA controllers treated it as missing possibly crashed, and NORAD says it did not hear about it until 9.24am.

The delay in responding to Flight 93's going rogue is equally astonishing. NORAD admitted being informed of its apparent hijacking at 9.16am, yet the Pentagon stated it had not yet intercepted the plane when it reportedly crashed in a Pennsylvania field a few minutes away from Washington, DC, at 10.06, some fifty minutes later.

There were no fewer than twenty-eight other air stations that, in theory, could have launched intercepts. The FAA ordered the 180th Fighter Wing out of Swanton, Ohio, to scramble their F-16 fighters at 10.01am. Although the base has no fighters on stand-by alert status, it managed to put fighters in the air an impressive sixteen minutes later, but still eleven minutes after the last hijacked plane had crashed.

A large station, Andrews AFB, lay just twelve miles south of Washington, DC. The Kean Commission Report (p. 44) says that "the first of the Andrews fighters was airborne at 10.38," ordered up by the Secret Service without NORAD's knowledge. They were almost exactly one hour too late to defend the Pentagon.

It remains a mystery why, with hijacked planes reported to be heading for Washington, nobody from the Pentagon asked Andrews to scramble jets. After 9/11 Andrews' website went down. When it went back up, links had been removed, which made it clear that despite some reports, it did indeed have "combat units in the highest possible state of readiness".[6]

Nine/Eleven skeptics say that the paralysis of the FAA, particularly the failure to report Flight 77 as a suspected hijacking, is clear evidence of the sort of tampering by high officials that either LIHOP or MIHOP scenarios would predict. They point to the FBI's threats to seek imprisonment for air traffic controllers talking to the press.

How could this paralysis have been achieved without alerting junior officials to a plot? In what the US media have described as a bizarre coincidence, NORAD – and, as we shall see, almost certainly the FAA – were in the middle of an exercise, code-named Vigilant Guardian, that might have had just this effect.

On the other hand, perhaps nineteen Arabs armed with knives just got lucky.

"Is This Real-World Or Exercise?"

It was a bright sunny morning after a national holiday, and American Airlines Flight 11 had taken off into crystal-blue skies. After responding to one routine instruction to adjust its course, a moment later it failed to respond to a second. There was no warning. No emergency code on the transponder. No single-keystroke hijack code on the ACARS. No shout on the radio.

At 8.39am Flight 11 passes directly over the number one terrorist target in the United States, Indian Point nuclear power station. The rogue aircraft could have caused a meltdown and a release of huge amounts of radiation. The Kean Commission claims that Binalshibh discussed the possibility but thought it lacked symbolic value. This is hardly "a new terrorist challenge, one whose rage and malice had no limit".[7]

Flight 11 was now in imminent danger of colliding with other airliners in these congested skies, but valuable minutes ticked by, between ten and twenty of them, as air traffic controllers tried to contact the plane. FAA regulations were perfectly clear. Any control tower monitoring a plane that had a transponder failure, made an unauthorized change of flight direction, or failed to reply to radio direction or questions from the ground was without fail to be treated as an emergency. Regulations stated that control towers should not allow any attempts to restore contact with the plane to last for more than four minutes. In the case of Flight 11 and Flight 77, air traffic controllers seriously overshot the time limits. Why?

USA Today's published route of Flight 11, based on Flight Explorer, shows the pilots diverting the aircraft towards Griffiss AFB, in Rome, NY. Home of the USAF's major communications and intelligence research laboratory, Griffiss bristles with state-of-the-art communications equipment. But according to the Kean Commission, a significant part of the route south towards New York is unknown and should be shown in dotted lines.

Copyright: USA Today/Flight Explorer

On September 11, NORAD was halfway through a week-long exercise, Operation Vigilant Guardian. NORAD's General Larry Arnold explained in his testimony to the Kean Commission: "I was handed a note that we had a possible hijacking at Boston center . . . (I asked) my staff, 'Is this part of the exercise?' Because quite honestly, and frankly we do hijacking scenarios as we go through these exercises from time to time . . . it had been a long time since we had had a hijacking, but the fact (was) that we had reviewed the procedures of what it is we do for a hijacking, because we were in the middle of an exercise. So we were pretty well familiar with those procedures . . ."

Does this sound like an exercise that "postulated a bomber attack from the former Soviet Union", as the Kean Commission

UA	09/11/2001	0171	UNKNOW	SFO	17:40	0:00	0381	0000	0	0:00	0000
UA	09/11/2001	0173	UNKNOW	SFO	19:40	0:00	0383	0000	0	0:00	0000
* UA	09/11/2001	0175	N612UA	LAX	8:00	7:58	0376	0000	-2	8:23	0025
UA	09/11/2001	0177	UNKNOW	LAX	18:55	0:00	0275	0000	0	0:00	0000
UA	09/11/2001	0199	UNKNOW	IAD	10:45	0:00	0090	0000	0	0:00	0000
UA	09/11/2001	0211	N463UA	IAD	7:45	7:39	0097	0085	-6	7:51	0012

This is the listing shown on the Bureau of Transportation Statistics' website for Flight 175 out of Logan International Airport on September 11 2001. However, no comparable listing is shown for Flight 11 on that day. The Kean Commission said that Flight 11 departed normally.

claims? At about this moment, Flight 11 had illegally changed course to fly towards Griffiss AFB, the USAF's major radar and intelligence center and NORAD's north-eastern command center.

Arnold's reference to the review of hijack procedures probably refers to new June 2001 procedures, which many 9/11 skeptics see as a smoking gun, amounting to a "stand down" order. The procedures state that permission from the Secretary of Defense is now required before planes could be scrambled. There are emergency exceptions but the new procedures, which contain confusing references back to other orders, would at least have caused hesitation at the Pentagon.

The left and right ACARS interfaces are located on the forward part of the center pedestal in this view of the cockpit of a Boeing 767. A single-key emergency code could be sent on the ACARS unit. An even faster method was to squeeze the radio button on the steering yoke and shout. How did the hijackers create mayhem in First Class of Flight 11 without alerting the pilots?

Conducting a combined anti-hijacking exercise on the symbolic date 9/11 (the USA's emergency telephone number for all rescue services) would appeal to the military mind, not Al-Qaeda, for whom it has no meaning. When Flight 11 failed to resume its filed course, come back on air, and restore its transponder, not only the unwitting air traffic controllers would be confused. At FAA HQ the managers of Vigilant Guardian would become aware that their exercise has gone wildly wrong, would be unsure what to do, and might be terrified of doing the wrong thing.

Was the conjunction of a terrorist attack, Vigilant Guardian, and the psychologically charged date of 9/11 all just a triple coincidence? Had terrorists somehow gained knowledge of the exercise and planned their operation to take advantage of it? Or was it part of a deliberate paralysis of US defenses, put in place to aid the attacks?

An exercise, to be completely realistic, might use real airliners that genuinely fail to respond and actually go off course. A number of other scheduled flights did go temporarily rogue that morning. The Kean Commission quotes one official: "9.27, Boston FAA reports a fifth aircraft missing, Delta Flight (19)89 – and many people have never heard of Delta Flight (19)89 [they got the flight number wrong]. We call that the first red herring of the day, because there were a number of reported possible hijackings that unfolded over the hours immediately following the actual attacks."

Were stressed-out air traffic controllers panicking, or were they responding to Vigilant Guardian, reporting instances of real airliners that had temporarily gone rogue as planned? Only the FAA's National Hijack Coordinator on that day could testify about that, but this is one of the many questions the Kean Commission ignores. However, the Kean Commission provides more support for this possibility again in its account of the Flight 11 crisis:[8]

At 8.37 Boston Center reached NEADS (the regional military command center). This was the first notification received by the military – at any level – that American Airlines Flight 11 had been hijacked.

> FAA: "Hi, Boston Center TMU [Traffic Management Unit], we have a problem here. We have a hijacked aircraft headed towards New York and we need you guys to, we need someone to scramble some F-16s or something up there, help us out."
>
> NEADS: "Is this real-world or exercise?"
>
> FAA: "No, this is not an exercise, not a test."

The Kean Commission says it is the first time the military has ever heard of Flight 11 going rogue. But in that case why would the military react in its very first comment that this might be part of an exercise? This could only happen, say skeptics, if the exercise involved hijacked aircraft. It would not happen if the military exercise merely involved Cold War scenarios of an attack by Russia.

In its final report the Kean Commission consigns Vigilant Guardian to a small-print footnote (Chapter 1, Note 116):

> On 9/11, NORAD was scheduled to conduct a military exercise, Vigilant Guardian, which postulated a bomber attack from the former Soviet Union. We investigated whether military preparations for the large-scale exercise compromised the military's response to the real-world terrorist attack on 9/11. According to General Eberhart, "it took about thirty seconds" to make the adjustment to the real-world situation. We found that the response was, if anything, expedited.

The likelihood of the "former Soviet Union" attacking the USA was close to nil and from its own evidence, as we shall see, the idea that NORAD was able to achieve anything on that morning "in about thirty seconds" is not credible. At this point, by the way, following the Flight 11 impact, the mass media channels were smoothly getting eye-in-the-sky helicopters into the air over the World Trade Center. Their routine mobilizations stand in stark contrast to the apparent impotence and indecisiveness of the $500 billion a year military.

On Board Flight 11

The NORAD exercise Vigilant Guardian provides some sort of explanation for the failure of the FAA to alert the US military. But what is the explanation for the failure of pilots to issue the hijack alert that would have ensured NORAD fighters were scrambled in time and could have prevented the hijackings of Flights 77 and 93?

One possibility is that the alerts were issued but ignored, as controllers assumed they were part of Vigilant Guardian. But all radio communications are recorded, so this would imply an unprecedented cover-up both by the FAA and the Kean Commission – dangerously proactive, highly illegal, and disastrous if discovered.

Space is cramped in the cockpit of a 767. In addition to the two pilots, four or even five hijackers locked themselves into this area, according to Flight Attendant Betty Ong.
Source: grantgilron@yahoo.com

Flight attendants Ong and Sweeney made two crucial phone calls from Flight 11 that supply all the gripping narrative provided by the Kean Commission. The media stated for months that Ong's long call was recorded, but only a four-minute recording of the lengthy call has been released by the Commission, saying that new machines could only hold the first four minutes of a call. Ong and Sweeney's accounts were praised by all for their calmness and professionalism, but they do not make sense.

How did the hijackers gain access to the cockpit? FAA rules required that the doors remain closed and locked during flight, but perhaps these were ignored. Ms Sweeney said that the alleged hijackers, in First Class, had stabbed two flight attendants and slit the throat of a business-class passenger, killing him. In addition, according to one account, an FAA memo produced on

The navigation instruments array on a Boeing 767 is recognizable to any instrument-trained pilot. The transponder switch is on the wall behind the pilot. Setting a course for the WTC would not have been difficult, assuming a nearby airport's directional data were known, but the automatic pilot, with its pre-programmed flight-plan route, would have had to be switched off.

September 11, they shot first-class passenger Daniel Lewin. All of this mayhem apparently occurred *before* the hijackers breached the cockpit, according to the Sweeney account.

It is reasonable to assume that stabbed flight attendants, as well as passengers, would have been screaming and shouting. Why did the pilots not alert ground control, given that there was a smell of mace, a possible gunshot, an outcry in First Class, and the cockpit was still free to communicate? At the very least, the pilot or co-pilot should have been able to send the emergency alert code, activated from no fewer than four places in the cockpit of a Boeing 767, including the steering yoke. Ong speculated that they had "jammed their way" in, but her call started when the hijackers were already holed up in the cockpit.[9]

The passengers are strangely absent from these accounts. According to the radio-telephone calls of the two flight attendants, all four (or five) of the hijackers locked themselves in the pilot's cockpit. Whether this is even physically possible or not, Betty Ong did not know "who's up there", and the eighty-one passengers apparently remained ignorant of the hijacking. They were only aware of "a routine medical emergency" in First Class that the cabin crew were calmly dealing with, in the Kean Commission's version.

It seems strange that passengers would remain totally compliant in spite of a former Israeli special forces member, Daniel Lewin, being either stabbed or shot to death in First Class, and flight attendants being killed or badly injured near the cockpit door. How did the horrified remaining cabin crew allay the passengers' fears, while tending the injured or making long calls on the telephones at the rear of the plane? Were the passengers all paralyzed with fear by the "bomb with yellow wires attached" that flight attendant Amy Sweeney said one of the hijackers brandished?

Nobody shouted or screamed in the background of the calls. Why were there no Airfone or mobile phone calls from Flight 11 passengers while the hijackers were "locked in the cockpit"? And why did the National Security Agency, which monitors all call traffic, not come up with the evidence? It's almost as if there are no passengers on Flight 11, as it flies low down the Hudson valley, past Indian Point nuclear power station, across Manhattan's unmistakable restricted airspace. Vital latter parts of the flight attendants' calls are not recorded. These correspond with the time when the aircraft was out of official view, its track only reconstituted later by Pentagon staff.

The official narrative holds that for the alleged hijacker's giveaway announcement – "We have some planes" – to be overheard by ground control, a switch was flipped by the pilot. The state of Massachusetts gave chief pilot John Ogonowski a posthumous award for this act. But if Oganowski could flip a switch to alert controllers to a PA system announcement, why could he not earlier have performed the momentary act of keying in the 7500 "hijacked" code or pressing the alarm button, thereby ending the controllers' apparent bafflement? Moreover, skeptics wonder, *why did the alleged hijackers not simply use the prominent handset supplied exclusively for the pilots' use in addressing the cabin?*

In June 2004 relatives of the victims were astonished to hear a new tape recording. Sweeney's call had not been recorded but the call to senior management relaying its details had been. Pledged to secrecy by the FBI, the relatives nonetheless passed on what they had heard to the *New York Observer*: "In Fort Worth, two managers in SOC [Systems Operations Control] were sitting beside each other and hearing it," says one former American Airlines employee who heard the tape. "They were both saying, 'Do not pass this along. Let's keep it right here. Keep it among the five of us.'"[10]

Why did American management not take appropriate action when they learned that the first hijacking in seventeen years had taken place on one of their airliners and the hijackers were boasting they had more aircraft? A likely explanation is that they thought it was part of the Vigilant Guardian exercises. Otherwise how could the managers possibly imagine they could keep this hijacking a secret?

Destruction of evidence is a familiar aspect of the 9/11 investigations. Only hours after the attacks, an enterprising New York FAA manager gathered the six controllers who dealt with the two hijacked planes, and recorded their personal accounts of what occurred for federal investigators. A second manager destroyed the tape between December 2001 and January 2002 by cutting it into small pieces and depositing the pieces in trash cans. His explanation: he had promised a union official representing the controllers that he would "get rid of" the tape after they used it to provide written statements to federal officials.[11]

Was there a gun on board? In a briefing issued by the FAA on the evening of the attacks, Suzanne Clark of American Airlines corporate HQ told the FAA that: "A passenger located in seat 10B shot and killed a passenger in seat 9B at 9.20am. The passenger killed was Daniel Lewin, shot by passenger Satam Al Suqami."[12] Later though, the then FAA boss Jane Garvey told the Kean Commission this was due to the "fog of war" and that the FBI had "found no evidence" of it. The Commission followed her opinion, but what evidence could the FBI have found in a crash where even the flight recorders were lost?

Were there box cutters? Jane Garvey denied any knowledge of them: "To the extent to which they were used or how they were used, I don't have that information." So the Commission asked the FAA spokesman: "Mr Mead, anything?" "No, sir." Nobody mentions the "bomb with yellow wires attached". In short, nobody knows what weapons the supposed hijackers had aboard.

A Soviet-Style White Elephant

The World Trade Center began in disaster, just as it ended. A grossly misconceived Soviet-style land-development catastrophe of the late 1950s that was obsolete long before it was finished, its Twin Towers symbolized everything wrong with modernism and the Rockefeller brothers who sponsored it.[13]

The oversized sixteen-acre site destroyed swathes of human-scale streetscape: five streets were closed off and 164 buildings demolished. The main towers exceeded 100 storeys simply out of greed for office space, and sixty workers died in their construction, not counting others who may have succumbed later to

WTC 1, the North Tower, is on the right, WTC 2, the South Tower, on the left. The enormous expense of building them could only have been borne by a public authority. Workers found the slim windows oppressive. Large amounts of asbestos left in both towers were a liability.

Copyright: Corbis

The replacement scheme is even taller than the World Trade Center, but tenants have been very slow to appear and its future is in doubt.

Copyright: Daniel Liebeskind

The Center consisted of two 110-storey office towers (One and Two World Trade Center), the often neglected forty-seven-storey office building (Seven World Trade Center) which stood to the north of them, two nine-storey office buildings (Four and Five World Trade Center), an eight-storey US custom house (Six World Trade Center), and the twenty-two-storey New York Marriott World Trade Center Hotel (Three World Trade Center). The World Trade Center Mall, located immediately below the plaza, hosted a wide range of shops and restaurants. The six basements housed two subway stations and a stop on the PATH trains to New Jersey.

asbestos spray. The top ten storeys were added to grab a brief highest-building status for PR purposes.

The buildings' owners, the New York Port Authority, did not pay full taxes to the City, and the towers' bad neighbourliness was staggering: they stole light from buildings all across Manhattan. Their exterior-frame structure cleverly maximized interior space while minimizing views and making office workers depressed. Space-saving on elevators that involved two changes up and down made for lengthy journey times: in the upper areas, unable to lunch out easily, workers stayed trapped all day. It would take a full two hours to evacuate everybody in a fire.

At the time, critics accurately called the towers banal, grandiose, boring, dreary, grim, vacuous, gross abstractions, and objects of extreme hubris. One of them called the windswept five-acre plaza at the base a "cement football field" and said it was never peopled during the buildings' entire thirty-year lifespan.

The WTC was not in great shape by 2001. The artificial dot-com boom was over and too much of the towers' 638,000 square metres of space languished empty. The towers were liable for a "mid-life rehab". However, the latest building regulations would have dictated stripping out the asbestos that still lined vast expanses of ceiling, not to mention the remainder that shielded all the 90,000 tonnes of steelwork in the North Tower and the lower third of the South Tower.

Such a job would have been unrealistically expensive and physically impractical, with no gain in revenues. For that reason, the place was pretty run down. To a tourist, the WTC looked like a rooftop photo-op, to an owner it might look more like a dead end. In summer 2001 the WTC had just changed hands for the first time.

Silverstein Property Corporation already owned number Seven WTC, the high-security tower that housed top-secret government offices, under a mortgage from the Blackstone Group. Now, boss Larry Silverstein had signed a new $3.2 billion ninety-nine-year lease on the Twin Towers, along with WTC 4 and 5, plus 37,000 square metres of retail space. Seven weeks before the center was destroyed, Port Authority officers handed over a giant set of keys to Silverstein.

Construction of the towers was simple. Faced with the difficulties of building to unprecedented heights, the engineers had copied the IBM building in Seattle. On the outside were closely spaced steel columns 41 centimetres wide and set only 48.4 centimetres apart, making the towers appear from afar to have no windows. On the inside was a massive central core. Each floor provided about one acre of office space.

A press release from the National Council of Structural Engineers' Associations after the 9/11 attack included a statement from Leslie E. Robertson, a member of the structural design team, that the towers had been designed to survive the impact of a Boeing 707. Aaron Swirsky, one of the fourteen architects on the WTC design team, told CNN the day following the attacks that he believed a plane would never have been able to bring the buildings down.

Like other skyscrapers, the towers had an emergency exit plan: in the WTC case it required approximately two hours for an orderly evacuation of the 50,000 occupants and roughly 4,000 visitors. Knowing this, the designers selected the best fire protection for the steel supports in the structure. That the towers eventually collapsed after being hit, and fell at such speed, not only astonished many engineers, it was unprecedented in the history of architecture. Some 9/11 skeptics have suggested that the towers were brought down by demolition charges placed either as part of the attacks or as part of a precaution to prevent the towers from toppling over. Even more baffling was the orderly collapse seven hours later of Silverstein's forty-seven-storey WTC 7, which had not been attacked at all.

Relatively Few Bodies

John Labriola worked for the NY Port Authority on the 71st Floor. He wrote an account of his escape:[14]

> It was pretty hot; people were slipping on the sweat of the people who had come before them. In some places the smoke was worse than others. Thank God the lights always stayed on. People covered their mouths and eyes with whatever they had available . . . Around the 35th floor we started meeting a steady stream of firefighters walking up and had to press into single file again. None of them said a word as they went up and past us carrying unbelievable loads of equipment . . . A few floors lower water was flowing creating rapids down the stairs. This got worse as we got lower down.

We learn from this account that the lights remained on and the sprinkler system was working. Firefighters felt they could handle the fires, and had confidence in the building.

A major issue for 9/11 skeptics is the mystery of how a fire that appeared to be generating more smoke than heat and which fire-fighters judged to be containable could lead to the collapse of the towers. But even with this "bonus" the attacks were hardly a great success for the terrorists allegedly involved. Indeed they seem almost designed to limit casualties.

Ramsi Yousef, convicted for the 1993 WTC bombing, said later that he had hoped to kill 250,000 people. Atta was supposed to have chosen morning flights for maximum slaughter but most people were apparently not at work yet. If he had chosen flights departing an hour or two later, using twice-as-big Boeing 747s, they could have killed thousands more than they did. Was the North Tower attack really one where "rage and malice knew no limit"?[15]

"The National Institute of Standards and Technology has provided a preliminary estimation that between 16,400 and 18,800 civilians were in the WTC complex as of 8.46am on September 11 . . . We can account for the workplace location of 2,052 individuals . . . only 110, or 5.36 per cent of those who died, worked below the impact zone."[16]

In the midst of the impact crater in the North Tower, where 10,000 gallons of fuel have recently ignited and a furious blaze is supposed to be eroding the entire structure, a woman stands tragically staring out.

Copyright: unknown

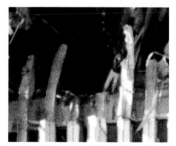

The stricken woman seems to be staring down at the world below. She has long, sandy hair, and wears a dark sweater and light blue slacks or jeans.

Link: http://911research.wtc7.net/wtc/evidence/photos/docs/woman_in_blackhole.jpg. Copyright: unknown

WTC 1, the North Tower, was the most lethal of the three strikes. Casualties could have been fewer if the New York authorities had briefed emergency telephone operators properly. "The FDNY ordered both towers fully evacuated by 8.57, but this guidance was not conveyed to 9/11 operators and FDNY dispatchers, who for the next hour often continued to advise civilians not to self-evacuate."[17]

In the South Tower, even more could have been saved: "No decision has been criticized more than the decision of building personnel not to evacuate the South Tower immediately after the North Tower was hit. A firm and prompt evacuation order would likely have led many to safety." As many as 600 could have been saved.[18]

Amateur photographer John Labriola captured this image of a hose-carrying fireman at about the 30th floor, hurrying up towards the impact point to extinguish the fires. Would highly experienced NY firemen have rushed up the tower if the fires were out of control and there were any remote expectation of it collapsing?

Credit: John Labriola

Evidence Found, Then Lost, Now Secret

In a case of mass murder, you might at least expect some clarity from the authorities on the question of the bodies. But in the 9/11 events, even that is missing. Dr Charles Hersh, the chief medical examiner, triggered an angry response when he told grieving relatives that many bodies – no one was sure how many – had been "vaporized" and were beyond identification.[19]

But Dr Michael Baden, the state's chief forensic pathologist, had opined at the time of the attack that most bodies should be identifiable because the fires did not reach the 3,200°F, thirty-minute level necessary to incinerate a body. Clearly the passengers' bodies could not have been incinerated into vapor, because Hersh reported about a year after the attack that thirty-three victims from Flight 11, and twelve victims from Flight 175, had been identified.

Further gruesome testimony that passengers had not been incinerated came from Chuck Allen, a WTC computer engineer, who reported a grisly discovery when he emerged into the plaza at the foot of WTC 1. Before him lay twenty, thirty, maybe forty dead bodies in pieces. "They saw a torso with a belt around its hip, a second, a third, a fourth. They were all wearing the same kind of wide black belt. It took Allen a moment before he comprehended that they had all been passengers."[20]

Were these the bodies that Dr Hersh later identified? How had the "wide black belts", originally anchored to airplane seats, been detached and remained with the bodies of passengers? Why had their bodies not been degraded in the blaze of 10,000 gallons of kerosene? Who had gathered these body parts together in the plaza?

Out of the 20,000 body parts eventually sifted from the ruins, two were identified as coming from the hijackers. The New York Medical Examiner's Office said the identifications had been made using DNA samples provided by the FBI from the steering wheels of vehicles

FBI official Barry Mawn said his men picked out a hijacker's passport from the sea of paperwork lying in the streets around the ruins of the towers on 13 September.

Copyright: Getty Images

hired by the hijackers and from hair samples recovered from their hotel rooms. The Examiner's Office said no names were attached to the two profiles that were matched to existing remains.

The Examiner's Office would not even say which of the four crash sites the anonymous "identified hijackers" came from. For 9/11 skeptics one reason for this unnecessary secrecy is clear: DNA from a named hijacker could be used to prove he was using a stolen identity.[21]

Little has caused more ridicule in the 9/11 saga than the apparent discovery of one of the hijackers' passports. There are two versions of this story. New York's FBI director Barry Mawn told CNN on 18 September 2001, that a "grid search" of streets surrounding the WTC had come up with several clues: "Last week, a passport belonging to one of the hijackers was found in the vicinity of Vesey Street, near the World Trade Center. 'It was a significant piece of evidence for us,' Mawn said."

On the other hand, CBS said the passport was found "minutes after" the attack (AP, 27 January 2003), while ABC News reported its discovery "in the rubble" on 12 September. Susan Ginzburg, senior counsel to the Kean Commission, stuck with the CBS version when she testified on 26 January 2004, that the passport of Flight 11 hijacker Suqami came from: "A passer-by [who] picked it up and gave it to a NYPD detective shortly before the World Trade Center towers collapsed."

Nine/Eleven skeptics suspect the passport was planted to help establish the official story in the first, critical hours. Unlike Flight 175, Flight 11 went right into the center of the building, no part of it emerged. They ask: how could the passport survive the inferno? And who found it and handed it in? With tens of thousands of foreign passport holders in New York, and well before the FBI had issued its infamous list of hijackers, why was it assumed the passport came from a hijacker? Why was it not filed as another piece of lost property? Barry Mawn was later promoted to FBI Assistant Director.

If investigators were lucky to find a delicate passport, their luck ran out when it came to the vital "black boxes". All large commercial airplanes are equipped with two of these, which are often orange or red. One is a cockpit voice recorder and the other is a flight data recorder. They record radio transmissions from the cockpit and flight information to help determine the cause of a crash. The recorders are located in the plane's tail, where they are most likely to survive. Impact tolerance of each unit is 3,400 Gs for 6.5 milliseconds, and fire resistance is 1,100°C for thirty minutes. Police found more than 20,000 fragments of human bodies in the ruins, but they were not able to find even one of the four instruments, each the size of a shoebox.

North Tower Hit:
Witnesses Report Explosions

Later we consider the evidence that the towers collapsed as a result of demolition charges, perhaps legitimately put in place as a precaution against a catastrophic sideways fall onto neighboring Manhattan. But well before the collapse there are several reports suggesting that high explosives might have been detonating already.

Could these explosions be explained by burning jet fuel and falling debris, or are they, as some 9/11 skeptics say, evidence the buildings were rigged with pre-set charges, some of which were prematurely triggered by the plane impacts and fires?

For the 1,360 people in the top nineteen floors of the North Tower, there was no escape after the rogue aircraft smashed into the 94th to 98th Floors at 8.46am. All three staircases were filled with debris. According to the Kean Commission: "a jet fuel fireball erupted upon impact, and shot down at least one bank of elevators. The fireball burst on to numerous lower floors, including the 77th, 50th, 22nd, West Street lobby level, and the B4 level and four storeys below ground. The burning jet fuel immediately created thick, black smoke, which enveloped the upper floors and roof of the tower."[22]

A video of 9/11 events made by the Naudet brothers – French film makers who happened to be following a firefighting crew around that day – does not support this statement. It is as if the Commission staff had never viewed the Naudet material (although they mention it on p. 544, Note 52).

The Naudets' camera follows their fire crew leader into the lobby, the first firefighter to arrive. A big man in a suit approaches him and the narrator states: "A guy from the Port Authority told him the damage was somewhere above the 78th Floor, but all you had to do was look around, it was obvious something had happened right there, in the lobby." In the video, the windows have been shattered and broken stone wall-panels lie around over a wide area, with fine, dry, light gray dust covering the whole place. There is none of the soot or oily residue that burning jet fuel would have left behind.

More evidence contradicts the Kean Commission account. Mike Pecoraro was an engineer working with a colleague in the lowest basement of the North Tower when the attack happened. They were told to stay where they were and "sit tight" until the Assistant Chief got back to them. By this time, however, the room they were working in began to fill with a white smoke. The two decided to ascend the stairs to a small machine-shop, but according to Mike, "There was nothing there but rubble . . . We're talking about a 50-ton hydraulic press? Gone!"

The two made their way to the parking garage but found that it, too, was gone: "There were no walls, there was rubble on the floor, and you can't see anything," Mike said. They decided to ascend two more levels to the building's lobby. As they ascended to the B Level, one floor above, they were astonished to see a steel and concrete fire door that weighed about 300 pounds, wrinkled up "like a piece of aluminum foil" and lying on the floor. Having been through the 1993 bombing, Mike recalled seeing similar things happen to the building's structure. He was convinced a bomb had gone off in the building.[23]

Pecoraro's name does not appear in the Kean Commission, although he worked on the maintenance staff, had been through an earlier bombing and was convinced a bomb had gone off again. A 50-ton hydraulic press blown away, a parking garage wrecked, a 300-

The fire in the North Tower rages on Floor 94, where the impacting aircraft's ruptured tanks spewed kerosene across the one-acre floor. The official report said the building did well to endure as long as it did, forgetting its previous survival of an office fire on several floors, and the fact that a steel-framed building had never before collapsed.

Copyright: unknown

pound steel and concrete fire door mangled up like aluminium foil: all these things suggest high explosives, and not just a kerosene fireball ninety-four floors up.[24]

Were these explosions caused by the fireball itself? This seems unlikely: according to the FEMA report: "Although dramatic, these fireballs did not explode or generate a shock wave. If an explosion or detonation had occurred, the expansion of the burning gasses would have taken place in microseconds, not the two seconds observed. Therefore, although there were some overpressures, it is unlikely that the fireballs, being external to the buildings, would have resulted in significant structural damage."

Reports of explosions were not confined to amateurs. In the days after the attacks firefighters agreed: "On the last trip up a bomb went off. We think there was bombs set in the building," one told the New York *People*.[25] After this, firefighters were forbidden by their chiefs from talking to the media.

4: A Second Aircraft Hits the South Tower

In contrast to the silent Flight 11, the passengers of Flight 175, the second flight to be hijacked, made several phone calls, according to the Kean Commission: "The (Flight 175) hijackers attacked sometime between 8.42 and 8.46. They used knives (as reported by two passengers and a flight attendant), Mace (reported by one passenger), and the threat of a bomb (reported by the same passenger). They stabbed members of the flight crew (reported by a flight attendant and one passenger). Both pilots had been killed (reported by one flight attendant)."[1]

No billing or recording evidence is offered for any of these phone calls, only an FBI crime file reference. Few issues have caused as much controversy amongst 9/11 skeptics as the passengers' apparent phone calls. These eyewitness reports were cited, for instance by Blair, as the proof positive the official narrative was true. A 2002 drama documentary was made for Granada TV around the evidence of what many referred to as the mobile phone calls.

Griffiss AFB at Rome, NY, is headquarters of NEADS, the NORAD north-east regional command and houses the USAF's major research and intelligence-gathering laboratory. When Flight 175 sighted Flight 11, the two planes were about 140 miles from Griffiss, where NORAD commanders were conducting Vigilant Guardian. Both airline pilots were ex-armed forces. The Kean Commission Report makes no specific mention of Griffiss AFB.

Copyright: USAF Global Security

There was just one problem: it is all but impossible to make a mobile phone call above 8,000 feet. When we queried Granada about this, the film's producer failed to return our calls. A researcher we tracked down said they had heard that such calls were impossible but they had not looked into it any farther.[2]

Ironically, the publication of the Kean Commission coincided with an announcement from airlines that they were introducing a new system to facilitate mobile calls from planes. The Kean Commission does not raise this issue and mostly refers to "phone calls" without specifying how they were made.

Let us return to Flight 175. As with Flight 11, the first to be hijacked, the Kean Commission skates over how the hijackers gained access to the cockpit without alerting the pilots and causing them to give the hijacking alarm. One obvious explanation is that NORAD's exercise, Vigilant Guardian, confused the issue. Perhaps air traffic controllers received the alarm and thought it was part of the exercise. Perhaps pilots had been briefed to switch off radios and modify the transponder message themselves, in order to test for a few minutes the response of the FAA and the military to a hijacking event. This was widely predicted by friendly intelligence agencies in summer 2001, as we have seen, and new procedures had been introduced in June 2001.

Of all the coincidences of the 9/11 events, one of the oddest is that Flight 175 and Flight 11, both piloted by ex-military men, crossed each other's paths at the same time. Of all the planes in the air over America it is Flight 175 that spots the hijacked Flight 11, nine minutes before it too is hijacked.

The pilots were asked to look for a lost American Airlines plane. Here is an edited transcript of the communications:[3]

> **Controller (8.37):** "Do you have traffic [?] look at uh your twelve to one o'clock at about, uh, ten miles southbound to see if you can see an American seventy six seven out there please."
>
> **UAL175:** "Affirmative we have him, uh, he looks, uh, about twenty, yeah, about twenty-nine, twenty-eight thousand."
>
> **Controller:** "United 175, turn five, turn thirty degrees to the right. I [want to] keep you away from this traffic."
>
> **Cockpit (8.41):** "We figured we'd wait to go to your center. We heard a suspicious transmission on our departure out of Boston. Someone keyed the mike and said: 'Everyone stay in your seats.' It cut out."

Transponder signal no longer received (8.46).

Controller (8.53): "We may have a hijack. We have some problems over here right now."

This exchange raises the further question of why the captain of Flight 175 did not report the "suspicious transmission" he had heard some twenty-seven minutes earlier, on departure.

At 8.42, Flight 175 veers off its authorized course. A controller apparently says: "looks like he's heading southbound but there's no transponder, no nothing, and no one's talking to him." However, the transponder is turned off for only about thirty seconds, then changed to a signal that is not designated for any plane on that day (*Newsday*, 10 September 2002). This "allow[s] controllers to track the intruder easily, though they couldn't identify it" (*Washington Post*, 17 September 2001). Three years later, a NORAD commander put it slightly differently, telling the Kean Commission that Flight 175's transponder was never turned off.

Some four minutes later, the pilot of US Airlines Flight 583 tells flight control, regarding Flight 175, "I just picked up an ELT [emergency locator transmitter] on 121.5 it was brief but it went off." The controller responds, "OK, they said it's confirmed, believe it or not, as a thing, we're not sure yet . . ." And ten minutes later a flight controller tells other airplanes in the sky regarding Flight 175, "We may have a hijack. We have some problems over here right now."

Once again, as in the case of Flight 11, we find that controllers seem to be unwilling to accept that planes that have lost contact and changed course should be treated as hijacked. Once again, the Kean Commission fails to investigate why, and once again, the explanation suggests itself: the controllers were confused by a hijack element in the Vigilant Guardian exercise. The controller for Flight 11 was also the controller for Flight 175.

Moreover, the Kean Commission reports this message at 9.01 from the New York FAA center, in whose airspace Flight 175 is now flying. Manager, New York Center: "We have several situations going on here. It's escalating big, big time. We need to get the military involved with us . . . We're, we're involved with something else, we have other aircraft that may have a similar situation going on here."

The Commission comments that: "The 'other aircraft' referred to by New York Center was United 175." But to 9/11 skeptics there can hardly be a better example of the Kean Commission's ability to misread evidence. Here he interprets "several situations" and "other aircraft" – both in the plural – as a reference merely to the uncertainties of Flight 175. Once again, the Vigilant Guardian hypothesis would be a far better explanation for this evidence.

A plane, apparently Flight 175, hit the South Tower at 9.03, but the head of Massachusetts Port Authority, operators of Logan (Boston Logan International Airport), told the Kean Commission that they were not able to establish for hours what had happened to it. Can confusion and panic really explain the fantastic delays and egregious errors made by the experienced professionals at the FAA in establishing which plane had hit the South Tower? Nine/Eleven skeptics see more evidence here of a hidden agenda, and scope for a plane swap along the lines of Operation Northwoods.

When Flight 175's pilot makes visual contact with Flight 11, flying ten miles to the south, both planes are about 140 to 150 miles from Griffiss AFB, near Rome, NY: home of the Pentagon's regional command center. The NEADS Sector Operation Command Center at Griffiss is "responsible for monitoring the skies above 500,000 square miles of the north-east".[4]

But Griffiss is far more than just an operational HQ. The USAF consolidated its four research laboratories into a single Air Force Research Laboratory at Griffiss in 1997. The base specializes in the development of technologies for command and control communications and intelligence systems, advanced computers and microchips, communication devices and techniques, software engineering, intelligence gathering and processing devices, surveillance systems, advanced radars, super conductivity, infrared sensors, cryogenics, artificial intelligence applications, and related technologies.

Griffiss has been central to radar research since before the Second World War. In December 1942 no fewer than 14,518 military and civilian personnel worked on radar at the laboratories. This was the brains of the exercise NORAD was conducting on that day – and NORAD still knew nothing of the whereabouts of Flight 11, a 'heavy' (the term used for a large aircraft) that was about 100 miles off course and heading towards New York City at eight miles a minute? Why does the Kean Commission Report make no mention of Griffiss and its extensive facilities?

Skeptics point out that if anyone in the US Government was planning a Northwoods-type plot for 9/11, Griffiss would be the perfect home for the X Team, the small covert team of in-the-know operatives. Reserve intelligence personnel from all three services train with state-of-the-art equipment and systems at the Joint Reserve Intelligence Facility of the Air Force Research Laboratory Information Directorate. This is co-located with the Information Directorate's Information and Intelligence Exploitation Division, which houses servers and workstations linking it to intelligence production centers worldwide.

The disappearance of Flight 175 over Griffiss left plenty of time for a rendezvous with another aircraft and replacement by it on the rogue flight course. Did the confusion enable an exchange of aircraft, some kind of Operation Northwoods-style rendezvous in the air? There was a lack of clarity for hours from the authorities over the identity of the plane that hit the South Tower.[5]

Was Norad's Radar Pointing the Wrong Way?

How much did the controllers at the FAA and the military at NEADS (based at Griffiss) know about the flight paths of the rogue planes, and when did they know it? Even with transponders off, the FAA should have been able to track the planes by primary radar systems.

NORAD told the Kean Commission the armed forces could not "see" the hijacked airplanes because their radar, as opposed to the military-linked FAA's, monitored the shore approaches to the north-east. Major General Larry Arnold (Ret.) of NORAD told the 9/11 Commission: "we couldn't see into the interior of the country, we couldn't talk to our aircraft that were airborne to the interior of the country, and we did not have a command and control system that would absorb the number of radars."

In simple language, the radar was pointing the wrong way. This is extraordinary, but few have questioned it in the Washington corporate media. It would seem to imply that if enemy bombers or cruise missiles could penetrate the US coastline they would be free to fly wherever they wanted within the US mainland, so long as they remembered to turn their transponders off.

However, the Pentagon's PAVE PAWS system boasts on its own website that it "does not miss anything occurring in North American airspace". It says it is "capable of detecting and monitoring a great number of targets that would be consistent with a massive SLBM (Submarine Launched Ballistic Missile) attack". How do we square this with NORAD pleading that it could not "see" any of the rogue aircraft throughout the nearly two hours of the attacks?[6]

NORAD told the Kean Commission that "much of this radar data for these primary targets was not seen that day. It was reconstructed days later (an article in *Airman* magazine said two hours[7]) by the 84th Radar Evaluation Squadron (RADES), and other agencies like it who are professionals at going back and looking at radar tapes and then, given that they are loaded with knowledge after the fact, they can go and find things that perhaps were not visible during the event itself." However, the *Airman* article said RADES did not find Flight 93 in the records. Could that apparent failure have anything to do with suspicions that Flight 93 was shot down?

These radar reconstructions are crucial to the Kean Commission's identification of which aircraft supposedly hit which targets. The Commission makes no attempt to identify the aircraft by part numbers or other debris found at the crash sites. In other words, the Commission bases its whole plane identification case on radar "reconstructions" supplied by the Pentagon.

One of the main arguments of 9/11 believers is that a major Northwoods-type hoax would be impossible to hide. But skeptics can make the case that the Kean Commission, on the basis of its cited evidence, could have been fooled in this vital area of evidence by a handful of operatives at RADES. These individuals could have been told an exercise had gone horribly wrong and the authorities wanted to avoid embarrassment. The only falsification needed might be to "lose" a few seconds of incriminating data, a "detail" which would probably be ignored by the ever credulous Kean Commission.

What Hit the South Tower?

The mass media confidently speak of Flight 175 hitting the South Tower and show maps of its route from Boston, but for many 9/11 skeptics this proves nothing. They point out that apart from the radar reconstructions from the murky depths of the Pentagon's intelligence sections, hard information about Flight 175's

A millisecond before the impact with the South Tower, something like a blast of flame appears at the nose of the attacking airliner, which seems to have some kind of bulbous housing attached beneath its fuselage just aft of the engines. This frame comes from CNN, and is taken from a video that was replayed over world television millions of times. But the "pod people" are ridiculed by others who argue the picture shows a highlight of the oval bodywork that links the 767's wing with the fuselage.

Copyright: CNN/Carmen Taylor

movements is scarce. For instance, the Kean Commission and news reports have a departure time of 8.00, and the plane taking off at 8.14, whereas Bureau of Transportation Statistics apparently show actual departure at 7.58 and take off at 8.24.

The flight recorders vanished at the crash site and there are no reports that anyone checked the plane parts found at Ground Zero. New York City's chief medical examiner, Dr Charles Hersh, stated that he had identified the remains of twelve of the passengers aboard Flight 175, but only after they went through the Fresh Kills facility. According to some skeptics, a small group from the plotters' X Team could have fed them into Fresh Kills from anywhere.

Radical Nine/Eleven skeptics have two separate scenarios in mind. On a Northwoods plan, the true planes might have been landed at Griffiss and replaced by remote-controlled substitutes. Alternatively, the original planes (with or without real hijackers) might have been taken over by remote control.

Military research has come up with unmanned jet aircraft, such as the US Army's Predator drone (one was shot down overseas on

Carmen Taylor, of Ft. Smith, Ark., poses with her digital camera in New York on Tuesday, September 11 2001. Sightseeing on a Manhattan vacation with her son's digital camera, Taylor photographed the jetliner crashing into the South Tower earlier in the day. One of her photographs showed the plane at an angle just before impact: it is visible on the camera screen.

Copyright: AP Photo/Robert Bukaty

9/11), Boeing's X-45A, the X-47A and Global Hawk, the latter two developed by Northrop Grumman.

Such systems are now commonplace in the military industrial complex. Well-connected conspirators would have little difficulty sourcing a sophisticated custom system that could be fitted to an airliner, or within one. For example, a very senior appointee at the Pentagon (and Northrop Grumman director) was formerly vice-president of Systems Planning Corporation, which offers a product called the Flight Termination System that controls an aircraft from several hundred miles away.

Some speculate that frequent hijackings in the 1970s and the introduction of "fly-by-wire" technology might have combined to motivate the aviation industry to find a classified method of overriding a rogue pilot in a jetliner, a policy that was publicly mooted in the days after the 9/11 events. Andreas von Buelow has even

Blow-ups from other videos show the same bulbous housing on the underside of the attacking plane.

Another video frame shows the pod.

However, this hazy video grab taken from the east shows no pod below the fuselage.

suggested that such systems are already in place. It is conceivable that a 9/11 Vigilant Guardian-type exercise could have involved the testing of such a system.

It has also been suggested that the mysterious crash of Egyptair Flight 990 in October 2000 over New York was a dry run. The crash killed over a dozen Egyptian generals who had just received expensive advanced training in the US. It was blamed by US investigators on a nervous breakdown by the pilot. Egypt has vehemently denied this, while the cockpit tape indicated the pilot had mysteriously lost control of the plane.

A USAF plane photographed at RAF Mildenhall exhibits a pod underneath its fuselage.

Some skeptics say that genuine hijackers (LIHOP), or covert operatives (MIHOP), could have been lured into a trap. They might think they were taking advantage of the NORAD exercise to stage a daring multiple hijacking. But instead of "going back to the airport" as a Flight 93 pilot was overheard announcing to the passengers, they might find the airliner failing to respond to cockpit controls, propelling them and everybody aboard towards unexpected martyrdom.

On any of these scenarios, there would be no fear of the substituted aircraft being identified in the ruins, because a police and air accident investigation did not take place.[8]

Fireball Fury For the Media

TV channels were able to get helicopters into the air to hover over the towers, but the $500-billion-a-year Pentagon said it was unable to get a single aerial vehicle to the scene. For the rogue pilots, whoever they were, the presence of the TV channels transmitting the blaze across the world, must have been the main purpose of the attacks.

The approaching airliner executed a sharp turn to impact the South Tower on the left side, catching it at an angle and partially emerging on the side facing the camera. Much of the (roughly) 10,000 gallons of kerosene, torn from the wing tanks, flew forward through broken-open walls to form an aerosol. It then ignited into a fireball, burning off harmlessly outside the building.

Here is napalm being deployed by the US Air Force. Some 9/11 skeptics say a drone plane was loaded with napalm to create a news spectacular.

5: The Towers Collapse

How did the Towers collapse so spectacularly and so completely? The Pancake Theory promoted by some experts asserts that temperatures were hot enough to cause the floors of the South Tower to fail, but eyewitnesses state the temperatures nearby were cool enough for them to walk away without the danger of being cooked alive. A suppressed tape of the firefighters, leaked a year after the attacks, confirmed the fires were already dying down when the collapse occurred.

The impact floors of the South Tower were 78 to 84. Donovan Cowan was in an open elevator at the 78th Floor sky-lobby: "We went into the elevator. As soon as I hit the button, that's when there was a big boom. We both got knocked down. I remember feeling this intense heat. The doors were still open. The heat lasted for maybe fifteen to twenty seconds I guess. Then it stopped."

After the North Tower shock, the occupants of the South Tower had just sixteen and a half minutes before a second jet, one looking like United Airlines Flight 175, would tear through their building. In that brief window of time, 2,000 people from those floors and above faced a critical choice: stay or go. They didn't know what was coming, but if they moved quickly enough, ignoring official instructions, they would survive.

Workers along the north and west sides of the South Tower could immediately see the seriousness of the smoke and flames in the North Tower. The sight of fifty or sixty people jumping to their deaths from the stricken North Tower to escape smoke and fire goaded them into evacuating. That shocking sight saved lives as witnesses fled in horror.

The South Tower shows fires caused by an aircraft impacting from the other side, while the North Tower fire ebbs.

Ling Young was in her 78th Floor office: "Only in my area were people alive, and the people alive were from my office. I figured that out later because I sat around in there for ten or fifteen minutes. That's how I got so burned."

Despite the massive volumes of smoke, firefighters who reached the impact zone thought the resulting fire was manageable. A lost tape of New York firefighters' voices indicated that firefighters climbed far higher into the South Tower than practically anyone had realized. At least two men reached the crash zone on the 78th Floor, where they went to the aid of grievously injured people trapped in a sprawl of destruction. The Chief of Battalion 7's assessment when he saw "two isolated pockets of fire" was that "We should be able to knock it down with two lines. Radio that 78th Floor numerous 10-45 Code Ones."

The voices, captured on a tape of Fire Department radio transmissions, betray no fear. "Two hose lines are needed," Chief Orio Palmer says from an upper floor of the badly damaged South Tower at the World Trade Center. Just two hose lines to attack two isolated pockets of fire.[1]

Until the building's final minutes, both men were organizing the evacuation of people hurt by the plane's impact. Both men died in the collapse. The Kean Report ignores the judgment of these professionals and simply records that, instead of being able to knock down the fires and thereby save 600 lives, "A ladder company on the 78th Floor was preparing to use hoses to fight the fire when the South Tower collapsed."[2]

The existence of the tape, owned by the Port Authority, was kept secret even from the Fire Department for months. Nearly a year after the attacks the Port Authority allowed relatives to listen to it, but only after signing strict confidentiality agreements. Subsequently, the tape – circulating more widely – was leaked in full to the website, The Memory Hole. The unlikely reason for withholding evidence that seriously undermines the official 9/11 story was that alleged hijacker Moussaoui was facing prosecution for a related offence.[3]

Reduced to Rubble in Twenty Seconds

Here is a trade tower, shown under construction in 1970. The solid concrete core takes up the majority of the space. It has forty-seven reinforcing box columns, each weighing as much as 2.5 tons per linear foot. The pillars are jacketed in asbestos.

Credit: FEMA

These two NBC video frames show the top thirty storeys of the South Tower tipping over, a few milliseconds apart. Below the break point, puffs of smoke or dust are either indicating pre-located explosives or a very even blast of air pressure from the collapse, which at this instant is only slowly gathering speed. In the second picture, the phenomenon is repeated. Further up the building, above the damaged columns, clouds of pulverized concrete also suggest an explosive force. Nine/Eleven skeptics ask: why would concrete pulverize so rapidly in the upper section?

Copyright: NBC TV

The impossible happens – a first in the 100-year history of steel-frame towers. "The South Tower collapsed in ten seconds ... The building collapsed into itself, causing a ferocious windstorm and creating a massive debris cloud," is the Kean Commission's entire commentary (p. 305), although it does mention a fire chief saying the South Tower had fallen because it was "hit on a corner". Below the impact point of the planes the

structure of the towers was virtually unaffected up to this moment. The core pillars had huge carrying strength, and yet the floors they supported fell almost as fast as if they were flying through thin air. Thousands of tonnes of tough concrete were changed in seconds into falling rubble and a fine dust cloud which, unfurling from the broken joint of the building, settled all over South Manhattan.

Copyright: Amy Sancetta

The Experts Can't Believe It

Professor Wilem Frischmann, of the Pell Frischmann Group and the City University, London, took part in the inquiry into the Ronan Point disaster (which did not involve a steel-framed building). "Prior to 11 September, I scarcely believed that this icon was vulnerable," he said. "My current analysis of the collapse sequence [suggests that] damage caused to the outside would not have triggered collapse." In a report replete with unanswered questions, Professor Frischmann said that sprayed-water fire protection should have maintained the buildings' internal strength for several hours.[4]

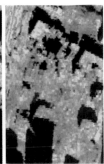

Thermal photos taken from the air by the US Government mapped dozens of hot spots in the WTC ruins. Construction-quality steel has a very high melting point of about 2,800°F (1,535°C). How could a fire based on kerosene, paper, or the other combustibles available in the towers, generate this much heat in an oxygen-poor environment? Thermite, a chemical compound used in demolition explosives, can produce just such temperatures, skeptics point out.
Credit: USG.S.

Michael Taylor, a demolition contractor from Pennsylvania who was certainly no 9/11 skeptic, told *New Scientist* magazine that: "The collapse of the WTC towers looked like a classic controlled demolition ... They could have tipped onto other buildings or into the river across the West Side highway."[5]

Van Romero is vice-president for research at New Mexico Institute of Mining and Technology (NMTech). He told the *Albuquerque Journal*: "My opinion is, based on the videotapes, that after the airplanes hit the World Trade Center there were some explosive devices inside the buildings that caused the

Instead of seeing WTC 6 pounded flat by the collapse of the Twin Towers, we see clearly where pressures in its basement have blown open two huge craters. FEMA concluded that it had been flattened by debris. There is no data from this site.

Credit: FEMA

towers to collapse" however Romero suggested Al-Qaeda had placed the explosives.

And Romero should know. He is a demolition expert and a former director of the Energetic Materials Research and Testing Center at NMTech, which studies the effects of explosions on buildings. Ten days later, however, Romero thought the towers could collapse. A recantation devoid of detail appeared in the same newspaper. The original report on the paper's web page now shows Romero's revised views first.[6]

The ongoing controversy flared up again when a laboratory director was fired in late 2004 after he wrote a letter to a NIST official challenging its melting-steel explanation of the WTC towers' collapse (AP, 11/23/04). Kevin R. Ryan worked at Environmental Health Laboratories Inc., a South Bend, Indiana-based subsidiary of Underwriters Laboratories, an independent organization that certifies product safety. Ryan said Underwriters Laboratories certified the steel used in the World Trade Center buildings, and questioned whether the fires in those buildings reached the necessary heat needed to melt bare steel. "The results of these tests appear to indicate that the buildings should have easily withstood the thermal stress caused by pools of burning jet fuel . . . This story (NIST's) just does not add up. If steel from those buildings did soften or melt, I'm sure we can all agree that this was certainly not due to jet fuel fires of any kind, let alone the briefly burning fires in those towers. That fact should be of great concern to all Americans. Alternatively, the contention that this steel did fail at temperatures around 250C suggests that the majority of deaths on 9/11 were due to a safety-related failure. That suggestion should be of great concern to my company."[7] However, Ryan's company denied it ever certified the steel in the World Trade Center buildings, according to AP.

Nine/Eleven skeptics point to the many cases – as illustrated by these examples – not of any dishonesty, but of the psychological power of the official story to make even experts doubt their own judgments. Time and again, we hear people essentially saying: Well my evidence is this, but because of what I have seen from other experts on other subjects on the mass media I realize I must be mistaken.[8]

Still No Official Explanation For the Collapse

The official story of how the towers collapsed was still a complete mess late in 2004. Journalists in the corporate media seemed to think the "Pancake Theory" popularized by The Discovery Channel is fact. The film, *How the Towers Collapsed*, promoted the view that, due to the heat, the floors collapsed one on top of another like pancakes, leading to the collapse of the columns.

The Pancake Theory arose when instant media wisdom – that damage to the structures had caused the collapses – had to be abandoned. Architects angrily insisted they had allowed for a Boeing 707 collision in their plans for the building. But the Pancake Theory says the damage was done, not by the plane impacts but by the heat of the fires. However, this also fails to address the architects' position, because the older Boeings had

In a blazing inferno at the Interstate Bank Building in LA on 4 May 1988, firefighters successively launched attacks on a raging fire from all four stairways onto the 13th, 14th, 15th, and 16th Floors. The fire gutted four floors in a sixty-two-storey steel frame building, but at no point did it threaten to collapse. Compare this also with the collapse of WTC 7.

Copyright: LA Fire Dept

similar amounts of fuel and were of a comparable size.

The Pancake Theory implies that the fire was much worse than any office fire the architects could have expected. The building was, however, designed with a high tolerance to fire, as it was recognized that evacuation would take an exceptionally long time. The core was fireproofed.

But how hot was the fire? There was indeed a lot of kerosene, but there was a comparably vast amount of steel, which has a very high heat conductivity, to absorb it. In any case, much of the kerosene aboard the planes seems to have vaporized and fireballed, burned off, or simply evaporated within about five minutes: so apart from the structural damage done by the plane, and predicted by the architects in their contingency planning, the situation should have been little different from a normal office fire.

Nine/Eleven skeptics have calculated that the entire 10,000 gallons of jet fuel from the aircraft, injected into one floor of the World Trade Center, and burned with perfect efficiency, would have raised the temperature of the floor to 536°F (280°C) at the most.[9]

The first building stood firm for an hour and a half after the attack, and no steel tower had ever collapsed as the result of an office fire. On 23 February 1975, the design had been put to the test: an intense fire broke out on the 11th Floor of the World Trade Center. The fire subsequently spread down to the 9th and up to the 19th Floors, but this fire did not cause failure of the floor trusses (nor any other major structural feature). A news report said at the time: "The fire department on arrival [at the World Trade Center] found a very intense fire. There were 125 firemen involved in fighting this fire and twenty-eight sustained injuries from the intense heat and smoke. The cause of the fire is unknown."

If the Pancake Theory makes no sense, 9/11 believers are left with the impact damage theory, in conflict with the buildings' architects. But the outside walls of the towers were undamaged for more than three-quarters of their perimeters, and the main load-bearing structure was in any case the massive central core.

The engineers most closely involved in the aftermath were Weidlinger Associates Inc., the New York City-based engineers who led the post-event study for WTC leaseholder Larry Silverstein. They took the view that as it could not have been the floors, it must have been the columns which failed. They decided that the initial hits destroyed thirty-three of fifty-nine perimeter columns in the north face of WTC 1. In addition, computer modelling showed that the impact of the plane also destroyed or disabled some twenty of forty-seven columns in the center of the core of WTC 1, they said.[10] But the damage described is asymmetrical. The collapse of the North Tower appeared symmetrical. The TV aerial on the summit of the structure sank vertically.

On February 12th, 2005, a 32-story steel-framed tower in Madrid the same age as the Twin Towers was engulfed in flames for days. Some top storeys collapsed, but the rest of the tower stayed standing.

Credit: Fox News

Weidlinger Associates had discredited the pancake theory, but was their own theory – the failure of the central columns – any better? According to one skeptic it ignored basic geometry.

"In the case of the North Tower, the trajectory of the plane took it right through the core, so between zero and four H-columns may have been taken out by the fuselage. The reason that a maximum of four core columns may have been taken out, is that the fuselage was sixteen feet, five inches wide and the core columns were spaced roughly twenty feet apart. Since the aircraft hit square on, at most one row (four columns deep) might have been impacted."[11]

The firefighters were also clear that a rapid pancake collapse was unthinkable. Deputy Chief Hayden told the Kean Commission: "We were completely unaware that the South Tower had collapsed. I don't think it was in our realm of thought." At a meeting with the Mayor of New York at the command center at 9.20am on the day, "none of the chiefs present believed a total collapse of either tower was possible."[12]

Chief Hayden's most detailed account confirms the view of many 9/11 skeptics: "We recognized the possibility of a collapse, but our thought process was that there was going to be a partial collapse, a gradual collapse after a couple of hours of burning, and we thought we had time to complete the evacuation and get everybody out. We made a conscious decision early on that we weren't going to try and put the fire out."[13]

But on this last point, Hayden was contradicted by his own Battalion Chief, who reached the seat of the fire in the South Tower – and deemed it easily controllable, as we saw earlier.

Unprecedented Disaster, Investigation Stymied

Why were the collapses of the towers and their forty-seven-storey neighbor, WTC 7, which was not struck by a plane, not investigated on the spot by professionals? The National Transportation Safety Board, noted for its thoroughness, objectivity and know-how with respect to large-scale disasters, could have led the investigations.

Somebody originally ordered all the metal from the fallen structure to be labelled. But eventually, from the whole 1.2 million-tonne pile, a derisory 156 assorted fragments were kept as evidence for investigators seeking an explanation for the buildings' collapse. The rest of the metal was shipped to the Far East for recycling.

Credit: Photo by Andrea Booher/FEMA News Photo

Instead, an ad hoc study group was sponsored by the Federal Emergency Management Agency and the American Society of Civil Engineers. Neither of them was an investigatory body. They did not have the full resources that might have been made available, nor did they control the site, which was managed by the Mayor's Office of Emergency Management and policed by the FBI. Very few experts were allowed on site.[14] Bechtel, the privately owned US conglomerate which employed Rumsfeld in the 1980s and would soon be massively involved in "reconstruction projects" in occupied Iraq, was retained for safety supervision on the WTC site.

The ferocious protection provided at the site was justified to defend the gold and drugs, computer records and body parts there, but skeptics observe that the evidence might have provided confirmation that explosives were used or even that the planes were switched.

The site teams at the towers were focused on rescue, retrieval and clean-up. The essential evidence needed to identify the cause of the collapse and intensity of the fire was lost. The vital structural steel pieces that could have told the full story were sold as scrap metal. Only 156 assorted pieces were retained. Had the NTSB been involved, the evidence would have been documented and protected. The NYPD improvised a crime scene at Fresh Kills, New Jersey, but the damage had already been done.

Credit: Photo by Andrea Booher/ FEMA News Photo

Demolition workers at the wreckage of the World Trade Center give an impression of girth of the steel lattice that encircled each tower. The supporting columns inside weighed up to 2.5 tonnes per foot.

Credit: Photo by Andrea Booher/ FEMA News Photo

Experts, seeing the site being cleared, started to complain. FEMA's engineering investigation into the Twin Towers' collapse was "woefully under funded", said James Lee Witt, who had led FEMA in the Clinton administration. He told *Newsday* that the $100,000 the federal government allocated thus far "wouldn't even make a dent". FEMA eventually allocated a mere $600,000 to fund the only investigation of the building collapses that functioned before the site had been mopped up.[15]

NIST's (National Institute of Standards and Technology) investigation was begun a year later, long after the evidence at the WTC site had been removed, and was strictly constrained. Although it was funded with a budget of $30 million, it worked on the premise of the official story, namely, that the collapses of the Twin Towers and WTC 7 resulted from the impacts of scheduled airliners. In its 7 May 2003 news release on the progress of its investigation, it seemed clear that the agency had been hampered in its investigation by a lack of access to evidence.

When NIST produced its interim report of the ongoing study on 18 June 2004 it said that, although no steel-framed building had ever before been brought down by fire, its working hypothesis attributed the collapses to just that – fire. "Fires played a major role in further reducing the structural capacity of the buildings, initiating collapse. While aircraft impact damage did not, by itself, initiate building collapse, it contributed greatly to the subsequent fires." Three years after 9/11, the experts were still going round in circles.

Bill Manning, editor of *Fire Engineering* magazine, articulated some of the professional indignation about the destruction of evidence at the time. "Except for … a three-day, visual walk-through of evidence sites … described by one close source as a 'tourist trip' no one's checking the evidence for anything," Manning told *American Free Press*. Manning issued a "call to action" to America's firefighters and fire engineers in the January 2002 issue to demand a blue ribbon panel to thoroughly investigate the collapse of the World Trade Center structures.

Manning challenged the theory that the towers collapsed as a result of the crashed airliners and the subsequent fuel fires, saying, "Respected members of the fire protection engineering community are beginning to raise red flags, and a resonating theory has emerged: The structural damage from the planes and the explosive ignition of jet fuel in themselves were not enough to bring down the towers."

No evidence has been produced to support the theory that the burning jet fuel and secondary fires "attacking the questionably fireproofed lightweight trusses and load-bearing columns directly caused the collapses", Manning wrote, adding that the collapses occurred "in an alarmingly short time".[16]

James Quintiere, Professor of Fire Protection Engineering at the University of Maryland, pointed out that fires could not have destroyed the Twin Towers and WTC 7. He lamented the recycling of the evidence, and called for a genuine investigation.[17]

The WTC 7 Collapse

Built in 1983 by the privately owned Tishman Corporation, builders of the Twin Towers, WTC 7 was a large building, reaching to forty-seven storeys, but was always overshadowed by the Twin

Fires show in the windows of WTC 7 at the 11th & 12th Floors. Otherwise, this façade is intact. The louvers serve the emergency generators under the 5th Floor. Mayor Giuliani and his team evacuated the "emergency operations" bunker in the building before the Twin Towers collapsed.

Copyright: Federal Emergency Management Authority (WTC 7 report)

WTC 7 microseconds before it collapsed. The north façade appears to be intact, as does the south side. Smoke billowing from the left of the building is deceptively mingling with the huge cloud arising from the ruins of the Twin Towers lying beyond.

Copyright: Frank Didik

The supposedly evacuated "emergency bunker" between the 24th and 27th Floors in WTC 7 could have provided an ideal vantage point to observe, control drone aircraft, or organize a controlled demolition of the towers.

Copyright: FEMA (number not available, possibly withdrawn from collection)

Evidence being removed from the WTC 7 site, one of the most important building collapse sites in the history of architecture. No pieces from WTC 7 feature among the 156 pieces of debris retained at the Fresh Kills crime site by FEMA. At this site, there was no sanitation reason for rapid removal, because nobody had died in the building but still the vital evidence in a unique structural collapse was rapidly destroyed.

Copyright: Site owner

This steel-framed tower stood nearer to the collapse of the Twin Towers than WTC 7 and sustained considerable damage. However, it did not collapse. WTC 7 did not sustain any visible impact damage, and yet it collapsed seven hours after the fall of the Twin Towers.

Copyright: Michael Rieger/ FEMA News Photo

Towers to its south. WTC 7 partly straddled an electrical sub-station that supplied the whole WTC site, along with emergency generators for its high-security tenants.

WTC 7 was not just physically at the center of New York's financial affairs, it housed the offices of some of the most sensitive agencies in the country: the US Secret Service, the Inland Revenue Service, the Department of Defense, the Central Intelligence Agency, the Securities and Exchange Commission (SEC), and the Mayor of New York's Office of Emergency Management (OEM), along with the head office of Salomon Brothers merchant bank. WTC 7 was a natural choice to house the sealed-off emergency bunker for the city administration that was completed in 1998, just three years earlier.

For such a sensitive structure, special security measures would be paramount in the minds of its owners, and some of its tenants. The large tanks of diesel fuel located five storeys above ground, although hard to ignite, might render the building vulnerable to a bomb attack. One measure that might come to mind, particularly after the 1993 attack on the World Trade Center, would be priming the building for controlled destruction in the event of a terror attack.

WTC 7 is "Pulled"

Most 9/11 skeptics see the collapse of the Twin Towers and the Pentagon attack as the two critical weak points in the official story, at least so far as the physical evidence goes. If the towers were brought down with explosives, they say, then the prior knowledge and involvement of people within the US Government is undeniable, because you cannot rig a building with explosives in an hour or two.

If it is proven that WTC 7 was brought down with explosives, they argue, given the failure of official sources to explain the Twin

The north side of WTC7 showed only a few small fires, of unknown origin since nothing impacted the building.

Credit: FEMA (in its WTC7 report, removed from FEMA's website)

Towers' collapse convincingly, plus the abundant prima facie evidence of a controlled implosion, the official story is hanging on a thread. That thread is the possibility there could have been a safety or security reason for the Twin Towers to be rigged with explosives.

Skeptics expect that this thread would break immediately. Apart from the question of whether such a plan was actually in place, there would be a public outcry that someone had ordered the collapse of the North Tower (if not both towers) with the loss of lives that might have been saved by a rooftop evacuation. There would also be outrage that the public had been systematically deceived as to why the towers collapsed. Demands from New Yorkers (already deeply suspicious that the Bush White House had "consciously" allowed the attacks to take place, would be irresistible for a real criminal investigation, not to mention the blizzard of lawsuits from the affected parties.

WTC 7 appears almost untouched by fire in photographs taken at the time, but Deputy Fire Chief Peter Hayden told *Firehouse* magazine (April 2002): "[In] the afternoon . . . we were pretty sure that 7 World Trade Center would collapse. Early on, we saw a bulge in the south-west corner between Floors 10 and 13, and we had put a transit on that and we were pretty sure she was going to collapse. You actually could see there was a visible bulge, it ran up about three floors. It came down about five o'clock in the afternoon, but by about two o'clock in the afternoon we realized this thing was going to collapse."

A steel-framed building had never collapsed before this day, ever, but Deputy Chief Hayden was now sure that WTC 7, with little if any visible damage and not ravaged with flames, was going to collapse.

Larry Silverstein, appearing on US Public Broadcasting System TV, had a spectacularly different account: "[The Fire Department] were not sure that they were gonna be able to contain the fire. I said, you know, we've had such terrible loss of life. Maybe the smartest thing to do is pull it. They made that decision to pull and then we watched the building collapse."[18]

Although the PBS documentary itself was listed as out of stock when we went to press, readers can check Silverstein's voice from the many websites who have stored a copy of the recording.

The timing of the tower's fall is significant: the entire world was reeling in horror at the felling of the Twin Towers. Video of

WTC7 collapsing, as captured on video and broadcast on TV. It sinks in perfect symmetry, exactly as if by industrial demolition.

Credit: CBS videograb

the attacking airliners was being aired continuously, to the exclusion of practically all else. The seven-second, tidy collapse of a high-security tower at 5.20pm towards the end of a difficult day was likely to attract little attention and indeed it did not.

However, for thousands of structural engineers, insurers, architects and firefighters it was very different. This high-security building, with its secret offices, was only the third steel skyscraper in history to collapse. The other two were the Twin Towers. Although any structural damage that did exist was asymmetrical (as mentioned by Deputy Chief Hayden), the building fell in an integral, orderly descent, leaving a tidy heap of rubble within its property lines, exactly as in a controlled demolition.

Skeptics ask why the Kean Commission Report makes no mention of WTC 7. If the tower fell because of the collapse of the Twin Towers, then it was a result of the terrorist attack, and warranted the Commission's attention. If its collapse was not connected to the terrorist attack, then this, in itself, warrants a major inquiry.

The rubble of WTC 7 – one of the largest structural failures in history – was pregnant with implications for the safety of all skyscrapers, their occupants, and emergency personnel entering them. Over strong objections from the fire protection establishment, the evidence was destroyed. Scrap vendors bought the steel and shipped it to the Far East. No pieces of torn metal structure marked "save" were kept at Fresh Kills crime scene.

The official investigation by the Federal Emergency Management Agency (which is not an investigative body) was inconclusive. Of the large tanks of diesel fuel for the emergency generators, which the mass media casually used as an explanation, it said only: "although the total diesel fuel on the premises contained massive potential energy, the best hypothesis has only a low probability of occurrence. Further research, investigation, and analyses are needed to resolve this issue." The only further research, from NIST, promises to blame invisible fires at Floor 5.

Electricity supplier Con Edison, in its suit against landowners the Port Authority, claimed the diesel tanks had blown up, which FEMA denied. Con Ed said the collapse of the South and North Towers of the World Trade Center within twenty-nine minutes of one another had triggered the fire that caused an explosion in the diesel tanks, bringing down the tower (*New York Law Journal*, 11/09/2002). Since all the evidence had been rushed away, the case was hard to decide.

FEMA's conclusion, published in May 2002, just after the last ruins had been scraped from the Twin Towers site, went as follows: "the specifics of the fires in WTC 7 and how they caused the building to collapse remain unknown at this time." This uncertainty over the cause of the collapse of WTC7 is one of the most striking features of the official account.

Lost in the Rubble

Clearly there was a major public sanitation problem at the WTC crash site. It was a grisly heap of human remains and in addition to that overriding problem, there had been an FBI office suite in the North Tower, and large drug seizures lay open to public view in the ruins. Financial businesses had been the main tenants, and

The fires in the Twin Towers posed a serious menace to the prestigious corporate properties that clustered around their feet, most of them banks with access to expensive litigators.

With the exception of some collateral damage in the immediate area, the collapse of the towers saved the corporate neighbors' properties from being hit by toppling towers, and the New York Port Authority from major liability suits.

money caches plus valuable information were at risk. Over one billion dollars in gold lay under the ruins. All this warranted strict security, and it was rapidly imposed.

By April 2002, 185,000 tonnes of steel had been removed from the site for recycling (*New York Daily News*, 16 April 2002). In all, FEMA estimated that 350,000 tonnes were shipped to the Far East. Only 156 fragments were retained (NIST said 236). However, in the early stages there seem to have been instructions to catalogue and retain a lot more evidence, possibly all of it, as we can see from the FEMA photographs that show data written on all the metal debris, as if it were going to be stored some-where for investigation.

In addition to the destruction of the structural evidence, there seems to have been suppression of aircraft debris at the site that was of interest to plane crash investigators such as the National Transportation Safety Board, which attended the scene. There was a singular lack of official zeal in establishing that the aircraft that hit the Twin Towers were one and the same jetliners as those that had taken off from Boston.

Bodies need very high temperatures for total cremation into powder, and the crashing aircraft, with the fires that followed, would probably not have achieved the destruction of a single body beyond positive identification. And yet, more than 800 people remain unaccounted for, in spite of a long and detailed forensic examination.[19]

With bodies vanished, nobody could ever be sure who piloted the colliding aircraft, or the condition of the people on board. Some forty five passengers and an unnamed couple of the alleged hijackers were said to have been identified by DNA, but even this evidence had been removed to a crime scene thirty-five miles away before it appeared.

A fireman who had completed a twenty-four-hour shift a week after September 11, dramatically put the official view: "You have ten-

storey buildings that leave more debris
than these two 100-storey towers …
Where the fuck is everything? Why
aren't we finding more bodies? Cause
it's all vaporized – turned to dust.
We're breathing people in that dust."[20]
But while this seems the case with the
concrete, it is a stretch to apply it to

Gold bars as stored in the WTC vault.
Copyright: unknown

the bodies or the black boxes which require far higher temperatures to turn to powder.

Some $230 million worth of gold was discovered in a lorry in a
tunnel under the Center in November 2001.[21] We have seen no
reports of other caches being found. However, Comex was reported
to have at least $950 million worth of gold stored in its vault under
the Center, and the fate of that haul remains unknown.[22]

Although the flight recorder boxes vanished, a lot of extremely
valuable disk-drives were recovered from the site. The FBI sent
the 400 drives to a German company, Convar, which used its special "blue laser" technique to restore the information from the
damaged media.[23]

A Reuters story from 16 December 2001 reported that: "Using
a pioneering laser scanning technology to find data on damaged
computer hard drives and main frames found in the rubble of the
World Trade Center and other nearby collapsed buildings, Convar
has recovered information from thirty-two computers that support assumptions of dirty doomsday dealings," in other words
insider trading on advance warnings of the attack.

On the 19th, Reuters quoted Richard Wagner, a data retrieval
expert at the company, saying that illegal transfers of more than
$100 million might have been made immediately before and
during the disaster. "There is a suspicion that some people had
advance knowledge of the approximate time of the plane crashes
in order to move out amounts exceeding $100 million," he says.

"They thought that the records of their transactions could not be traced after the main frames were destroyed."

In June 2002, Ontrack/Convar was acquired by Kroll Inc. (Kroll, O'Gara, Eisenhardt), a major security firm that has strong ties to the US intelligence community. Anja Legg of Convar Deutschland told an email inquirer on 21 February 2004 that the result of the restoration project had been "rated as confidential by the Head of the US investigation team".

The Reuters' report of "other nearby collapsed buildings" presumably refers to WTC 7 which, as we have seen, housed the offices of the Securities and Exchange Commission, where share transactions would be monitored for suspicious spikes. The Kean Commission ignored this possible clue to the perpetrators of the 9/11 events. Widespread claims of insider trading in stock options in the week before the attacks were relegated to a footnote, with the assumption they referred to Al-Qaeda fund-raising (Kean Commission Report, p. 172 and p. 499, Note 130). No mention was made of winnings that were still reported to be unclaimed.

The World's Biggest Crime Scene

The hugely expensive – and in theory meticulous – salvage operation seems to have lost piles of crucial aircraft parts, lost or failed to find four six-ton aircraft engines, and failed to find two flight data recorders and two cockpit voice recorders. How did this situation arise?

Fresh Kills is a stream and freshwater estuary on the west of Staten Island, thirty-five miles south of Manhattan island, but its name is now notoriously linked to Fresh Kills Landfill, which covered 2,100 acres and was so large it could be seen with the naked eye from space. First opened as a "temporary" facility in 1947, Fresh Kills became the largest landfill site in the world. Of dubious legality, it operated under a series of federal consent

FEMA Coordinating Officer Ted Monette stands with an unnamed NYPD officer behind part of an aero engine at the Staten Island landfill on 16 October 2001, in FEMA's own photograph. The following February, the FBI announced through Associated Press that the amount of aircraft debris found at the WTC site was too small to be quantifiable. This big engine part was a vital piece of evidence about the identity of the attacking planes. Where did it go?

Credit: FEMA

orders, was unlined, and leached many tonnes of toxic chemicals and heavy metals into nearby estuaries each day. Its stink reached into neighbourhoods on both sides of the Arthur Kill, which separates Staten Island from New Jersey.[24]

This reeking and polluting dump was where the authorities resolved to create a major crime scene by depositing 1.2 million tonnes of evidence from the wreckage of the World Trade Center.

Bechtel, which supervised overall safety in the operation, is a privately held contracting colossus and a huge contributor to Republican (and to a lesser extent Democratic) campaign coffers. It had dealt extensively with the Saddam Hussein regime in the Reagan years, but when that relationship soured, two top board members became cheerleaders for the upcoming invasion of Iraq.[25]

Bechtel's directors included CEO Riley Bechtel, on the President's Export Council, advising on trade issues, Bechtel senior counsel and board member George Shultz, who was chairman of the advisory board of the Committee for the Liberation of Iraq, and General (Ret.) Jack Sheehan, senior vice-president at Bechtel, and a member of the influential Defense Policy Board.[26]

Also involved in the clean-up task was AMEC, the company that

In February 2002 workers shift the heaps of debris at the Fresh Kills crime scene, run by the New York Police Department, thirty-five miles south of the location of the WTC. Detectives and other workers spent months sorting and sifting through the rubble, using specially constructed mechanical sieves. Although 20,000 body parts were reputedly found here, none of the fluorescent orange, shoebox-sized flight recorders emerged.

had renovated and reinforced the stricken segment of the Pentagon and which would share with Fluor a $500 million contract to renew Iraq's power generation facilities.

Fresh Kills crime scene was run by New York Police Department (NYPD). "The FBI supports and runs the federal investigative areas and the NY Dept of Sanitation runs the landfill. Corps involvement with landfill began in early October," the US Army Corps of Engineers (USACE) reported. The Corps provided

Somebody demarcated this aircraft wheel that fell into the street, but later the number of aircraft parts found by the FBI at the Fresh Kills crime site thirty-five miles away on Staten Island was so few that they were "hard to quantify".

site management and administration, equipment support and inventory, and health and safety planning and enforcement, along with private contractor Phillips & Jordan (P&J).

The P&J directors went to view the WTC site on 14 September, noting that: "Among the debris were munitions, firearms and bags of street drugs that had been in the custody of an FBI office, (and) piles of aircraft and elevator parts," according to P&J

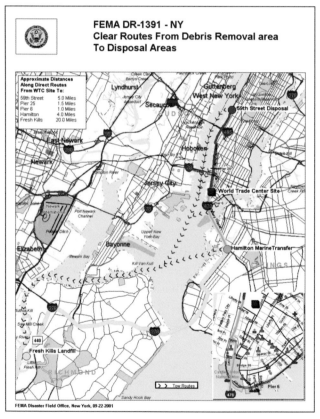

FEMA's disposal routes map showing the way from the WTC site in south Manhattan to Fresh Kills crime scene. Note Newark airport (left) where doomed Flight 93 took off.
Credit: FEMA

Executive Vice-President Patrick McMullen.

The company found it had nothing to do at the WTC site, and instead it was assigned to Fresh Kills, where 140 acres were devoted to operations, and another thirty-five to the sundry support buildings – from a mess hall to a medical tent – serving some 1,200 workers who took part in the effort. Incoming debris, most of which arrived via barge, had to be unloaded and trucked a short distance to the heart of the recovery site.[27]

First, large objects were separated out before further processing. These presumably included the "piles of aircraft and elevator parts" referred to by Patrick McMullen. Then screens and conveyors segregated the rest of the material and took it to NYPD detective-staffed "picking stations" for the removal of personal and evidentiary items of smaller sizes. The processing lines were Corps-built conveyors with shelters built around them for protection from weather.[28]

P&J planners devised a process whereby larger debris – steel girders, crushed automobiles, and the like   was separated from the rest via huge cranes (thirty-one in all, some of them 300 feet tall) and grapple excavators. The remaining tons of rubble were sifted through multi-level metal "shakers", consisting of layers of sieve-like plates, each plate with sifting holes smaller than those of the one above it. Materials that measured less than six inches in any dimension were ultimately divided according to size into three sub-groups, then run through screeners on a conveyor belt. At every stage, the separated materials were subject to new screenings and walk-through inspections. Human remains were taken to a temporary morgue, tagged and refrigerated for later DNA analysis. Even the smallest items of personal property were removed, photographed and catalogued by the New York Police Department in hopes of returning them to families of victims.

But hundreds of New York police officers and federal agents working from 5.00am to midnight every day never came across

FEMA engineers noted this "portion of the fuselage of United Airlines Flight 175" on the roof of WTC 5.

Credit: FEMA

A pedestrian photographed this piece of mechanical debris, apparently from a jet engine, on the pavement near the WTC site.

Credit: 911research.com

the shoebox-sized flight recorder boxes of the two airliners. "It's extremely rare that we don't get the recorders back. I can't recall another domestic case in which we did not recover the recorders," Ted Lopatkiewicz said on behalf of the National Transportation Safety Board.

The "piles of aircraft and elevator parts" that had been one of the outstanding features of the wreckage for Patrick McMullen had somehow disappeared. "So little [airplane] debris has been recovered that there's really no way to quantify it," FBI spokesman Joseph Valiquette told AP on 23 February 2002.[29]

For 9/11 believers the disappearance of the aircraft parts and failure to find the black boxes is just a detail, but for skeptics it shows that evidence that could have put doubts to rest has inexplicably vanished. Once again, this could have been accomplished, not by a vast conspiracy, but a small detachment from the X Team.

Removal of the large pieces of evidence could have occurred at the top of the evidentiary chain, where "larger debris-steel gird-ers, crushed automobiles, and the like was separated from the rest via huge cranes." Crane-drivers, few in number, could have been instructed to put "the like", namely aircraft parts, to one side for special attention in the "federal investigative areas".

Other reports of retrieved aircraft parts include the wheel that was photographed, the engine that was also photographed then apparently disappeared, the discovery in a building adjacent to the WTC, at 130 Cedar Street of "racks that held the luggage from one of the hijacked planes", and in a building at 90 West Street of "large sections of one of the hijacked airplanes".[30]

A normal inquiry would want to check the presumed airliner has the correct series number that identifies it from the factory production line. The 767 has over 620,000 individual parts. The engines have serial numbers that can be matched with the series number. Wiss, Janney, Elstner Associates Inc., of Chicago, Illinois, were paid $500,000 to reassemble TWA Flight 800 after it crashed into the sea in July 1996. No similar contract was awarded in the World Trade Center affair.

6: Flight 77: Shrouded in Mystery

As we have seen, the official account of Flight 11 and Flight 175 is dependent on the Pentagon's radar reconstructions, plagued with unanswered questions and marred by lost evidence. But for skeptics this is nothing compared to the story of Flight 77.

Video evidence apparently showing hijackers passing through security clearance before boarding Flight 77 was published on the same day as the final Kean Commission Report (21 July 2004). The video was sourced to litigators representing relatives of the

Associated Press released this video frame that they said came from litigators representing the bereaved families. AP's captions reads: "Hijacker Khalid al-Mihdhar, wearing the yellow shirt, foreground, passes through the security checkpoint at Dulles International Airport in Chantilly, Va., Sept. 11 2001, just hours before American Airlines Flight 77 crashed into the Pentagon in this image taken from a surveillance video." The caption makes three assumptions, but it was broadcast worldwide as corroboration of the official story.

Copyright: AP

A typical security video, as shown here, automatically identifies the camera (lower left), the location (lower right) and the time (upper right top) and date (lower right top). Any video without this information is suspect. Because this was a "leak" nobody had authenticated the video but the AP faithfully relayed the claims as facts.

deceased passengers, who were suing American Airlines for damages. The lawyers or the media themselves were piggy-backing this evidence on the report.[1]

The video was obtained by AP, which supplies news and newsroom equipment, not only to the whole US mass media, but to 3,300 TV stations all over the world, reaching a billion people. But skeptics say that while there is no evidence the video is forged, there is little evidence that it is genuine either, and see a similar process of validation by repetition as that which occurred over Iraq's alleged WMD. Once again, say skeptics, there is no vast conspiracy here, just an assumption that what officials say off the record is necessarily true.

Precisely where did this video come from ask 9/11 skeptics? Buried deep in the Kean Commission Report (p. 452, Note 11) are references to a video described as "Metropolitan Washington Airports Authority videotape, Dulles main terminal checkpoints, Sept 11 2001". But a normal security video has time and date burned into the integral video image by proprietary equipment according to an authenticated pattern, along with camera identification and the location that the camera covered. The video released in 2004 contained no such data.

Even if these pictures do portray the people they are supposed to, and are authentic surveillance shots, there is no proof of where they were taken. The Kean Commission reported that the hijackers made many flights. The video could show the men passing through security at any one of scores of airports.

The Kean Commission leaves unanswered the question of how the hijackers seized Flight 77. Indeed it is hard to see how the muscle hijackers could even have smuggled knives onto the plane. All four were subjected to individual inspections and all got through.

No potential weapons appeared on the "Dulles" video footage during the inspection of the suspects and their baggage. There was no sign of the notorious box cutters, which were banned by airline industry rules but approved by the FAA at the time. These suspects do not appear to be carrying any weapons at all to confront Captain Chic Burlingame, the Pentagon reservist piloting Flight 77 . . .

The Disappearing Plane

According to the Kean Commission Report, American Airlines Flight 77 just could not be found on the world's most sophisticated radar system after its transponder was switched off. They say one air traffic control center (Indianapolis) was looking in the wrong way, while the other (Washington) was never told that, with the transponder off, they needed to look for the primary radar trace. Meanwhile, the Air Force had no idea the flight was

Flight 77 pilot, Captain Chic Burlingame, was a decorated Vietnam-veteran Navy officer with Pentagon connections. Skeptics think he was an unsuspecting part of that day's confusing multi-agency exercise. He may have followed classified orders to switch off his own transponder, and cut radio contact as part of a Pentagon-organized test of the FAA and NORAD's systems. Why, otherwise, did he fail to issue a hijack warning when mayhem is supposed to have broken out in First Class and marauders broke into his cockpit?

Copyright: military.com

This Flight Explorer aircraft situation display shows Flight 77's pilot taking off at 8.21am, responding to a command about 100 miles out, then at 8.57 abruptly falling silent. The aircraft was out of official view for thirty-five minutes, as the Kean Commission Report admits (although it believes the radar reconstructions supplied by the Pentagon showed it was there all the time). No airliner identification evidence has been produced. Skeptics say that what happened in between remains open to question.

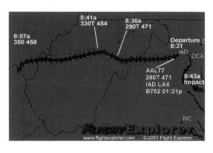

Credit: USA Today

anything other than crashed. And anyway, the radar systems didn't work properly in that sector.[2]

When the plane's transponder was switched off at 8.56, the Kean Commission states that the air traffic controller "did not know that other aircraft had been hijacked" but instead "believed American 77 had experienced serious electrical and/or mechanical failure, and was gone". An aircraft crashing while at cruising speed and clear of mountains is of course a highly unlikely event by any standards, but the controller took the serious step of launching an air and ground search for a downed aircraft.

If the individual controller was supposed to be unaware that aircraft had been hijacked that day, we are also told that supervisors and managers at Indianapolis FAA and even other agencies were also unaware. According to the Kean Commission: "Shortly after 9.00, Indianapolis Center started notifying other agencies that American 77 was missing and had possibly crashed . . . By 9.20, Indianapolis Center learned that there were other hijacked aircraft, and began to doubt its initial assumption that American 77 had crashed."

Author David Ray Griffin[3] wonders whether the Indianapolis controllers were on the right track, and Flight 77 had indeed vanished. He cites *USA Today* reporting in this regard that the FAA's

Jane Garvey notified the White House that there had been another crash.

What about American Airlines? When they learned a quarter of an hour after the crash of Flight 11 that Indianapolis had lost contact with Flight 77, also an LA-bound flight, this was the dialogue as reported by the Kean Commission:

Indianapolis to AA at 8.58am: "We were talking to him and all of a sudden it just uh . . ." to which AA replied immediately: "O.K., all right we'll get a hold of him for ya." Four minutes later, in response to Indianapolis, AA said: "yeah, 111 cell called him but I did not get a reply back from him." They parted with this exchange: "Yeah, we have no radar contact and, uh, no communications with him, so if you guys could try again." AA at 9.02: "We're doing it." The tower called again at 9.09: "Did you get a hold of American 77 by chance?" "No sir."[4]

By 9.02 all the news channels were showing the burning North Tower. Even if this was initally viewed as an accident, at 9.03, the second plane crashed into the South Tower. It is odd that no one considered the possibility of any connection at 9.02 or even at 9.09. It is even odder when viewed with the knowledge that by the time the alarm was raised about Flight 77, Amy Sweeny had spoken of the hijacking of Flight 11 to the AA System Operations Control in Fort Worth – although that was news which according to an article in the New York *Observer*, they had decided to keep "just between the five of us."

Losing track of a heavy (airliner) for ten minutes should have been a major emergency for American Airlines. Kean Commission staff recount more delay: "At 9.09, they reported the loss of contact to the FAA regional center, which passed this information to FAA headquarters at 9.24." The crashes on the Twin Towers should have eliminated any doubt as to what was going on, but FAA HQ remained paralyzed until at least 9.25 when a new man on the job at Command Center (he started that day) took the initiative and grounded all planes. Thus an organization, which according to the Kean Commission had operated with extraordinary lethargy at every juncture, also apparently handled an "unprecedented order" with "great skill", mass-landing 4,500 aircraft without incident.

As with Flights 11 and 175, how are we to explain the uncanny silence of the airline pilots? Again, as with Flights 11 and 175, American 77's pilot, Captain Chic Burlingame, was ex-armed forces – US Navy in his case. He flew F-4s during the Vietnam War, left active duty and went into the Navy Reserves in 1979, and served for many years as a liaison at the Pentagon. He started flying as a pilot with American Airlines in 1979 and retired from the Navy Reserves in 1996. The *Washington Post* reported that he once worked on anti-terrorism strategies at the Pentagon.[5]

Did Burlingame himself switch off the transponder and fail to give the hijack signal, or send a single-keystroke ACARS alert, because he was obeying confidential orders as part of the Vigilant Guardian exercise? This would also explain the peculiar first two lines of dialogue above, where AA controllers tell air traffic controllers they will contact Flight 77 before even waiting to hear any details of what has gone wrong.

Explaining Flight 77's disappearance from radar screens, the Kean Commission Report introduces yet another of 9/11's many coincidences: "for eight minutes and thirteen seconds, between 8.56 and 9.05, this primary radar information on American 77 was not displayed to controllers at Indianapolis Center." The lucky hijackers had managed to take over Flight 77 without the alarm being raised and in a "geographical area" where real-time primary radar tracking was impossible.

The Commission's words, buried on page 460 in Footnote 142 are a masterpiece of obfuscation: "the 'preferred' radar in this geographic area had no primary radar system, the 'supplemental' radar had poor primary coverage, and the FAA ATC software did not allow the display of primary radar data from the 'tertiary' and 'quadrary' radars."[6]

The Kean Commission claims baldly that: "American 77 traveled undetected for thirty-six minutes on a course heading due east for Washington, DC." By the time the suspected Flight 77 was spotted by Dulles (i.e. Washington) air traffic control, nobody was sure what the incoming radar blip was. Griffin quotes Danielle O'Brien, one of the air traffic controllers at Dulles who reported seeing the aircraft on screen at 9.25 (the Kean Commission claims it was 9.32) saying: "The speed, the maneuverability, the way that he turned, we all thought in the radar room, all of us experienced air traffic controllers, that that was a military plane." The Kean Commission does not report any interview with Ms O'Brien.[7]

The only other evidence produced by the Kean Commission indicating that the object that hit the Pentagon was indeed Flight 77 is its claim, on page 9 of his report, that "At 9.29 the autopilot on American 77 was disengaged." This information may have come from the flight data recorder, supposed to have been recovered at the crash site at 4.00am (sic) a few days later. The FBI director said at the time that "some information" was recovered from the flight data recorder.

Skeptics say the Kean Commission could have solved the whole matter by producing evidence of Flight 77 debris from the Pentagon crash site, but on that subject, their report is silent.

What Hit the Pentagon?

"At 9.37 American Airlines Flight 77 crashed into the Pentagon, traveling at approximately 530 miles per hour," states the Kean Commission Report on page 10. The support for the Commission's statement relies on reconstructed primary radar

The flight from Dulles International Airport to the Pentagon is only thirty miles, a matter of four or five minutes in an accelerating airliner. There would have been little time for the authorities to detect or defend against such a speedy attack. Instead, the official story puts Flight 77 in the air for nearly an hour and twenty minutes, risking interception for about forty-four minutes of the flight. This map shows a kink in the route. Did the legitimate pilot comply with operation Vigilant Guardian by deliber-

ately going off course? Was the plane downed somehow over remote hill country, as Indianapolis air traffic control decided when it launched an air and ground search?

Copyright: mapquest or copyright NAVTEQ

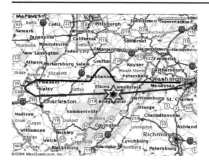

Flight 77's transponder signal ceased identifying the flight and its altitude on controllers' radar screens at 8.56am, thirty-six minutes after it took off. No hijack signal was given. An aircraft of some kind was seen hitting the Pentagon about forty-four min-utes later. For hours the mass media did not connect Flight 77 with the Pentagon crash. FOX News even said the Pentagon had been hit by a mil-itary aircraft. Reuters first reported a helicopter crash, which was validated by AP. Military sources

then built up the connection between Flight 77 and the crash, until by next day it had become part of the legend.

Copyright: Mapquest or copyright NAVTEQ

An unidentified aircraft reportedly approached Washington, DC, from west-southwest at about 7,000 feet. Eyewitnesses and air traffic controllers (following it on their screens) saw it descend rapidly and execute a 330-degree turn. Barely above the ground, it approached the Pentagon up the traffic-filled Highway 395, swerved left at the last minute and crashed into the west side of the Pentagon, killing fifty-five uniformed people out of a total 20,000 personnel.

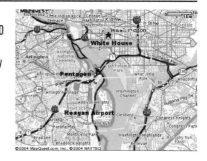

Copyright: Mapquest or copyright NAVTEQ

information supplied to the National Transportation Safety Board by the Pentagon, and a brief entry in an annual safety survey. There is no aircraft debris cited in this crash that helped launch the war against terrorism.

The Armed Forces Institute of Pathology eventually claimed it identified the remains of all the passengers' bodies (except a toddler), but this did not include the hijackers. DNA matches with the man known as Hani Hanjour should have been available – he reportedly lived in the USA on and off for as long as ten years.[8]

Of course, the hijackers may have been omitted as a matter of policy (which would also explain why they do not appear on the planes' passenger manifests released to the media). But the Kean Commission is anxious to validate the official story – for instance, there are two full chapters on the movements of the hijackers – so why did it not confirm hijackers' DNA matches with the authorities and report them to the public?

Was Hanjour really the pilot? CBS reported that the attack route's "complex manoeuver suggests the hijackers had better flying skills than many investigators first believed". There are plenty of witnesses to Hanjour's lack of competence as a pilot of small planes, e.g. from the *LA Times* (27 September 2001): "Hanjour, always an uncertain pilot, showed up at flight school in Bowie, Md. Three times, he attempted to rent a plane. Each time, a different instructor took him on a test flight and deemed him incompetent to fly alone." A month before the hijackings, the manager of the flight school said Hanjour could not handle basic air manoeuvers.[9]

Skeptics ask if this could really have been the same pilot who executed advanced aerobatics in an unidentified aircraft over Washington, DC, on September 11, 2001, descending from 7,000 feet to 15 feet (sic) in a tight, banking 330-degree circuit?

And why did the alleged hijackers not seize the plane on take-off and hit their target within minutes? Why did they instead fly for over half an hour, risking interception all the way, and make a lengthy circuit near the Pentagon missile system and the Secret Service's missile launchers at the White House, only in order to hit the sole unoccupied wedge of the Pentagon at its most fortified point? The Kean Commission Report, with its battery of small print notes accessing piles of official documentation, is silent on these points.

How Did Mrs Olson Call Her Husband?

Barbara Olson was a hawkish right-winger and CNN TV pundit, third wife of an even more hawkish right-winger, Ted Olson. Olson was appointed Solicitor General after he had persuaded the Supreme Court to appoint George W. Bush to the presidency by a margin of one vote.

The Olson phone call from Flight 77 was crucial in establishing the existence of marauders on a civilian flight and their possession of dangerous weapons. Later, the identity of the plane that hit the Pentagon hinged on it, too. The story has three versions in media reports and a fourth version in the Kean Commission. Each one is different.

CNN reported on 12 September at 2.06am Eastern Daylight Time: "Barbara Olson, a conservative commentator and attorney, alerted her husband, Solicitor General Ted Olson, that the plane she was on was being hijacked Tuesday morning, Ted Olson told CNN. Shortly afterwards Flight 77 crashed into the Pentagon . . . Ted Olson told CNN that his wife said all passengers and flight personnel, including the pilots, were herded to the back of the plane by armed hijackers. The only weapons she mentioned were knives and cardboard cutters. She felt nobody was in charge and asked her husband to tell the pilot what to do."

NOTES TO CHAPTER 1   455

24, 2003); Linda Povinelli interview (Sept. 24, 2003); see also NTSB report, Air Traffic Control Recording—American Airlines Flight 77, Dec. 21, 2001; AAL record, Dispatch Environmental Control/Weekly Flight Summary for Flight 11, Sept. 11, 2001.
   55. Gerard Arpey interview (Jan. 8, 2004); Larry Wansley interview (Jan. 8, 2004); AAL record, System Operations Command Center (SOCC) log, Sept. 11, 2001.
   56. FBI report, "American Airlines Airphone Usage," Sept. 20, 2001; FBI report of investigation, interview of Ronald and Nancy May, Sept. 12, 2001.
   57. The records available for the phone calls from American 77 do not allow for a determination of which of four "connected calls to unknown numbers" represent the two between Barbara Olson and her husband's office (all family members of the Flight 77 passengers and crew were canvassed to see if they had received any phone calls from the hijacked flight, and only Renee May's parents and Ted Olson indicated that they had received such calls). The four calls were at 9:15:34 for 1 minute, 42 seconds; 9:20:15 for 4 minutes, 34 seconds; 9:25:48 for 2 minutes, 34 seconds; and 9:30:56 for 4 minutes, 20 seconds. FBI report, "American Airlines Airphone Usage," Sept. 20, 2001; FBI report of investigation, interview of Theodore Olson, Sept. 11, 2001; FBI report of investigation, interview of Helen Voss, Sept. 14, 2001; AAL response to the Commission's supplemental document request, Jan. 20, 2004.
   58. FBI report, "American Airlines Airphone Usage," Sept. 20, 2001; FBI report of investigation, interview of Theodore Olson, Sept. 11, 2001.
   59. See FAA report, "Report of Aircraft Accident," Nov. 13, 2001; John Hendershot interview (Dec. 22, 2003); FAA report, "Summary of Air Traffic Hijack Events: September 11, 2001," Sept. 17, 2001; NTSB report, "Flight Path Study—American Airlines Flight 77," Feb. 19, 2002; Commission analysis of radar data.
   60. See FAA report, "Summary of Air Traffic Hijack Events: September 11, 2001," Sept. 17, 2001; NTSB report,

Incredibly, the Kean Report claims all Flight 77's outgoing phone calls reached an "unknown number". Skeptics thought it was the latest example of the contortions officialdom goes through in order to avoid the billing evidence on Barbara Olson's calls from the plane to the US Department of Justice.

This was the first detailed eyewitness account of hijackers to reach the public. A TV celebrity had seen them.

The Olson call is the only passenger story from the rogue aircraft that establishes the use of "cardboard cutters" or box cutters. It makes that inscrutable reference to Mrs Olson feeling that "nobody was in charge" and implies that the ex-Navy pilot and his co-pilot must have relinquished the controls and allowed themselves to be "herded" to the back of the plane with everyone else. Burlingame was a decorated war veteran and long-time Pentagon liaison officer. What advice could Ted Olson possibly offer him?

Tony Mauro of the *New York Lawyer* published a second account of the call a few days after the 9/11 events. This contemporary story fails to name the person who took the original call. It also differs on a key point from the official story: Mrs Olson "called on her cell phone from aboard the jet":

It was just as the World Trade Center attacks were unfolding that someone in the solicitor general's office took a phone call from Barbara Olson. Ted Olson's longtime assistant, Helen Voss, raced into the S-G's (solicitor-general's) office to tell them that Barbara was on the line, sounding panicked. He picked up the phone and exclaimed, "What, you've been hijacked?" She was calling on her cell phone from aboard the jet, which had just left Dulles Airport. Voss says, "My heart sank". The call ended abruptly, but then Barbara called again, reportedly asking her husband, "What should I tell the pilot?" . . . The pilot, along with the rest of the passengers, had apparently been herded to the back of the plane.[10]

Six months later, a third account appeared (apparently unpublished in the United States) when Ted Olson told the *Daily Telegraph*:

> She had trouble getting through, because she wasn't using her cell phone, she was using the phone in the passengers' seats . . . I guess she didn't have her purse, because she was calling collect, and she was trying to get through to the Department of Justice, which is never very easy.
>
> She wanted to know, "What can I tell the pilot? What can I do? How can I stop this?" I tried to find out where she thought she was – I wanted to know where the airplane was and what direction it was going in, because I thought that was the first step to being able to do something.[11]

These accounts of the call had the skeptics puzzled. How were the calls made? Early reports mentioned a cell phone but Ted Olson later thought she had used the Airphone in her seat. American Airlines Boeing 757s were not equipped with in-flight satellite phones for passengers. A call by us to American Airlines' London Office produced a definitive statement from Laeti Hyver that 757s do not have Airfones. This was confirmed by an email from AA in the US. Also if other seats had phones, why did no one else make calls?

Could she have used a cell phone? According to AK Dewdney, a Canadian academic and long time *Scientific American* contributor, successful mobile connections are unlikely from an airliner at cruising altitude. He hired a small plane in an experiment that showed mobile handsets' efficacy diminished with altitude. Over 8000 feet, he found, connections were rare.

Also, if mobile phones worked at that altitude, why would American Airlines invest in a new system to enable mobile calls? In the summer of 2004 *New Scientist* reported on this "Passengers could soon make cell-phone calls during a flight using onboard transceivers currently being flight tested." A satellite and a dedicated ground level gateway feed the tiny 0.6 watt phone transmission into the terrestrial network.

The Kean Commission did not say whether the calls were made on cell phones, passenger Airphones or staff Airphones. But the last of those options raises a further question. If there were useable staff Airphones, Barbara Olson may have used that for her calls as the Kean Commission account might imply, but why did Renee May call her parents and ask them to contact AA with news of the hijack? Why didn't she call AA herself? Why didn't anyone else use those phones to call AA? Also, if the FBI believe all four calls from Flight 77 were made between the Olsons, how did Renee May make her call?

Smack Into the Safest Place of All

Luckily for the Department of Defense, the person guiding the unidentified aircraft that hit the Pentagon chose to attack Wedge 1, which was meant to be unoccupied. Lucky also that according to the Kean Commission, Osama bin Laden was urging the attacks take

The three-quarter-ton floor-to-ceiling blast windows remain intact in the third storey. This was the only segment of the Pentagon so equipped.

Copyright: Steve Helber, AP

It's clear in this picture how much more vulnerable the Pentagon was to a crash on the roof than on its newly reinforced exterior wall. We are told that a part of the airliner, possibly the nose cone, possibly one of the engines, passed through this blast wall, concrete floors, and three-quarter-ton windows, to penetrate five more interior walls and emerge from a "punch-out hole" just below the walkways (bottom left).

Copyright: Department of Defense

place without delay. "Wedge 1 was just five days from completion . . . A portion of the building at the point of impact withstood collapse for nearly thirty-five minutes thanks to the newly installed reinforced structural steel and blast resistant windows, allowing thousands of personnel in the area to escape . . . Only 125 Pentagon personnel of the 2,600 people in the vicinity were killed." The uniformed personnel figure was fifty-five.[12]

A magnified view of the punch-out hole. Could that be aircraft debris, piled into a heap at the bottom of the picture?

Copyright: Department of Defense

The plane hit the least threatening place to life and limb in the whole vast building. "Loss of life was further prevented because both Wedge 1 and Wedge 2 were partially occupied, with Wedge 1 being populated following its renovation and Wedge 2 being vacated so renovation could begin. In all, the two wedges at full occupancy can accommodate 10,000 personnel; however, only 4,600 resided in the combined two million

The nose of the airliner is one of the softest places on the plane, and apart from the apparently false trajectory, it is hard to believe that one of the engines could have penetrated this far into the armoured building. Is the aperture not too large? Skeptics argue that only a missile could have penetrated this far with such power.

Copyright: Department of Defense

square feet when the plane pierced the building's historic facade." In fact, far fewer were in Wedge 1, which was supposed to be unoccupied for another week.[13]

Most of the deaths had an accidental, fluky quality: "When a colonel plotted where his co-workers stood at the moment of impact, using a large schematic of the second floor drawn by the Pentagon's renovation team, he found fatalities bunched in Lt. Gen. Timothy J. Maude's (recruitment) office suite, and in a section of the big room where the floor buckled. Outside those clusters, the dead were scattered without pattern; some people directly in the plane's path escaped, while others did not."[14]

AMEC, the UK-based multinational engineering firm that works with big oil conglomerates worldwide, did the original Wedge 1 renovation and reinforcing of the walls. Selected on the basis of a best-value proposal, AMEC served as general contractor for this $150 million renovation. It was still in charge of the site at the time of the attack. In fact, it handled everything concerning the first renovation, including sensitive telecommunications and information installations.[15]

After the 9/11 events AMEC was chosen for the no-bid two hundred-odd million dollar contract "as a nod to AMEC's high-quality work". More rewards duly came AMEC's way: "in early 2004, Fluor Corp. announced that its joint venture with AMEC had been awarded a no-bid contract worth up to $500 million . . . for construction, rehabilitation, operation and maintenance of power generation facilities throughout Iraq." In March 2004 AMEC's joint venture received a further contract, worth $1 billion, to rebuild water and sewage facilities in Iraq. AMEC was one of the very few UK companies to get business in the US/UK-occupied war-torn oil state.[16]

After the Pentagon attack, the Department of Defense said the Pentagon's renovations had behaved superbly in withstanding the force of the impact. But if, as the Pentagon told the Kean

Commission, their main worry was a cruise missile launched from abroad, 9/11 was pretty bad news. An airplane – not designed to penetrate anything – had punched itself in an apparently dead straight line through the outside wall, many internal reinforced concrete columns, a further five exterior brick walls, possibly a concrete floor, and come out the other side.[17]

As it happens, any X Team operatives would have had considerable opportunity to deal with unwanted evidence around the site, if they needed it. "Once outside, commanders and supervisors counted their people. Police told people to get away from the building. 'Another plane is inbound,' they shouted." Where did this information come from ask skeptics?

When the floors broke cleanly away from Wedge 2, leaving undisturbed office furniture and computers exposed on the upper floors there, another delay occurred. "The portion of the Pentagon to the right of the initial impact area collapsed. Firefighters withdrew until the situation stabilized." Here was another break for any X Team operatives. "Again at 10.15, the incident commander ordered a full evacuation of the command post because of the warning of an approaching hijacked aircraft passed along by the FBI. This was the first of three evacuations caused by reports of incoming aircraft."[18]

The Pentagon: the Attacks Were a Failure

Corporate TV, and later the Kean Report, depicted the presumed hijackers as bloodthirsty religious fanatics, but from the carnage point of view the 9/11 events were unsuccessful, as we have seen. About 54,000 people worked in the Twin Towers or were visiting during office hours, and fewer than 2,600 were killed or disappeared (*Newsday*, 4/6/2002).

The area of the Pentagon highlighted in red (left) represents the small proportion of the structure where the wall was newly fortified, and the interior sparsely occupied. The reinforced wall was easily identifiable by the construction equipment and cable reels parked directly outside it. While

other exterior walls dated from 1943, the exterior wall at Wedge 1 had recently been blast-reinforced using the latest tough concrete, new steel and Kevlar-cladding, with the addition of coated floor-to-ceiling blast-window units, each weighing three-quarters of a ton. Fifty-five military people died, but they represented a tiny fraction of the 4,600 in the area, and the 24,000 working in the building. The White House is an easy target across the Potomac river; the Secretary of Defense's office is on the opposite side of the building.

Copyright: Department of Defense

The alleged hijacker, with his desire to inflict maximum casualties, could have dive-bombed the roof of the prominent river-view wedge at maximum speed from 7,000 feet, thereby killing thousands of the hated enemy and possibly the Secretary of Defense. Instead he overflew and returned, executing a difficult, steeply descending circuit over the restricted flight zone of central Washington, DC, and in range of the Secret Service-operated missile defenses of the White House. After two and a half risk-fraught minutes his aircraft ended up aligned with the slim portion of the Pentagon that was newly armoured (highlighted in red).

Copyright: Department of Defense

At the Pentagon there were over 20,000 staff, of which 125 were killed or reported missing. Of a total of 68,000 target victims, fewer than 5 per cent lost their lives. Considering that the criminals who allegedly set out to create mass casualties successfully ploughed three airliners into symbolic monuments that were also prominent places of work this must be rated as a failure. Some 9/11 skeptics see this as evidence the attacks were engineered by US officials to be a "wake-up call" and hence as harmless as possible consistent with a spectacular show (MIHOP). Or, they were allowed to happen (LIHOP) and somehow minimized, perhaps because a key organizer was a double agent.

They Saw It, But Where Is It?

The Pentagon told Congress that "The Boeing 757 struck Wedge 1 on the Heliport side of the Pentagon very low to the ground and entered Wedge 1 just to the north of Corridor 4 on the first and second floors. The plane traveled through the Pentagon at roughly a 45-degree angle to the face of the building. It went through Wedge 1 and into the un-renovated Wedge 2 before exiting the C-ring, the third ring of offices, and into a roadway (A/E Drive) that circles the perimeter of the Pentagon between the B- and C-rings. According to federal investigators, the fully fuelled plane was traveling at 350 mph when it struck the Pentagon."[19]

The ground-level entry hole is confirmed by photos of the fire before the façade collapsed. But an examination of photographs of the crash site just after the impact challenges this account. Could an airliner really "penetrate the building's second story" without either opening a big crater or blowing back piles of debris onto the lawn? The hole was arguably large enough to draw in the fuselage, but what happened to the engines and wings, not to mention the tail which would have reached most of the way to the roof?

No trace of wings or tail-plane can be seen in front of the crash site.

Copyright: Department of Defense

An early CNN report had correspondent Jamie Mcintyre saying "From my close-up inspection, there's no evidence of a plane having crashed anywhere near the Pentagon. The only site, is the actual side of the building that's crashed in. And as I said, the only pieces left that you can see are small enough that you pick up in your hand."[20]

With no large holes in the façade, where did all the fuel go? A lot must have stayed outside. The fireball was immense (if the Pentagon video is to be believed) but assuming it was an inefficient combustion, once it subsided there should still have been hundreds, if not thousands, of gallons of burning kerosene in front of the Pentagon, of which there is little sign.

There have been contradictory explanations for the single hole and apparently missing debris. Some say the wings were pulled back through the hole or flung forward into the hole. But 9/11 skeptics invoke elementary mechanics, saying the massive forward momentum of the engines and fuel tanks would barely be affected by any momentary thrust the plane's relatively weak frame could transmit: they must have continued to move forwards and could not have made the sharp, almost instantaneous turn needed to fit through the single hole.

Different journalists writing for *The Times* and *Sunday Times* have stated that the plane was vaporized in the fireball, but one leading skeptic, *Scientific American* columnist A.K. Dewdney, has argued that not nearly enough heat was generated to turn the tail to vapor.[21]

Some of the eyewitnesses – including the Secretary of Defense – referred to "an explosion". Some described an explosion and a strong shock wave. Such a shock wave cannot be explained by the combustion of jet fuel, and suggests the detonation of an

This computer reconstruction gives some idea of how an airliner could have hit the Pentagon, but it does not solve the mystery of how its shattered bodywork vanished into the building, particularly the tail-plane, which should have hit the third storey, where blast windows remained intact, but no debris bounced back on to the lawn.

Credit: Silent But Deadly

The area behind the reinforced wall in flames after the murderous impact. A "more planes coming" scare was delaying the rescue operation around this time. The newly reinforced wall and its three-quarter-ton blast windows had sustained the impact, and would stand for about another thirty minutes, although the roofline was visibly sagging. The lawn is unmarked, and there appears to be no blow-back debris from the wings, tail-plane or rear fuselage. How did a 116-tonne 757 disappear into the Pentagon through a double-window-width cavity? What happened to the engines? There is no sign of one to the right of the hole and no hole for it to have passed through. Perhaps it impacted the wall, smashing limestone fascia blocks to the immediate right of the flames in the window and shattering. If so, it has disappeared from photos and indeed from the public records.

Copyright: US Army (Cpl James Ingersoll)

This shot, taken by the photographer of the Army Secretary, shows a pristine lawn in front of the crash site, suggesting that the airliner impacted at such speed that almost the whole plane somehow entered the building, or that it "vaporized" as the media have explained.

Copyright: Sgt Carmen Burgess

explosive. Detonation waves may come from kerosene, ignited in aerosol form, but they are comparatively weak. Several witnesses with the benefit of military experience smelt cordite, an explosive compound used in aircraft gun ammunition. Cordite N is cool-burning and produces little smoke and no flash, but, like other explosives, produces a strong detonation wave.[22]

Smoke and Mirrors

In an evident attempt to answer skeptics who did not believe it had been hit by Flight 77, or even by a jetliner, the Pentagon released to Associated Press on 7 March 2002 video stills taken from the CCTV camera at the heliport car-park on 9/11. But the frames only raised more questions. Some skeptics think they are completely faked, because the brilliant white explosion casts no shadow towards the camera and the time data on the video frames is wrong. Others take them as valid and see abundant evidence there was no plane the size of a 757.

Why are the authorities refusing to divulge the contents of three other videos, both of which they seized? The FBI confiscated video footage from a nearby gas station, a rooftop camera on the nearby Sheraton Hotel tower, and from traffic surveillance cameras on Highway I-395. For skeptics, the fact that video content from all three locations has been kept secret throws the Pentagon story into doubt. It certainly seems hard to square with George W. Bush's statement to the United Nations on 10 November 2001, when, invoking the "many thousands [who] still lie in a tomb of rubble", he said, "Let us never tolerate outrageous conspiracy theories concerning the attacks of September the 11th; malicious lies that attempt to shift the blame away from the terrorists themselves, away from the guilty."[23]

Sep. 12, 2001, 17:37:19   plane

Compare the height of the Pentagon's seventy-foot wall (right of center) with the 155-foot length of a Boeing 757 that should be there. Where is it? The attack plane, its tail fin visible at the right top of the right-hand control box, looks far too short. The tail fin itself looks too small. A white smoke trail is visible behind the plane. However, jet contrails only happen at high altitudes when the water vapor from a jet's exhaust freezes into visible ice crystals. The only explanation of this white smoke (apart from an air vortex) is that it is the rocket-engine trail from a guided missile.

Sep. 12, 2001, 17:37:19   impact

The missile conclusion is supported by evidence in the second image, where the initial fireball is the white flash explosion consistent with a small missile warhead. There is no similar white flash in the WTC collision photographs. On the other hand, the flash should cast a shadow from the pillars towards the camera and some have pronounced the film a fake.

Sep. 12, 2001, 17:37:21   #2 impact

The hazy engine trail lingers over the lawn, as the impact explosion turns a rich red.

A Costa Rican, operating a gas station with a good view of the crash, said he had never seen his CCTV footage. According to Bill McKelway of the *Richmond Times – Dispatch* (11 December 2001): "Velasquez says the gas station's security cameras are close enough to the Pentagon to have recorded the moment of impact. 'I've never seen what the pictures looked like,' he said. 'The FBI was here within minutes and took the film.'"[24]

Evidence and Eyewitnesses

Pictures of aircraft debris at the Pentagon are few, just as they are at the World Trade Center crash site. Here we publish the clearest ones we have been able to find. They point to some kind of aircraft having crashed into the Pentagon, but whether it was Flight

The Pentagon's theory is that the front of the plane compacted, effectively turning into a hard bullet, and finally emerging here. The punch-out hole *might* show a piece of nose fuselage (left), and a forward landing wheel hub (right). If the rest of the fuselage and cockpit was ever there it has been removed. It seems surprising that the pieces of metal show no signs of blackening from fire.

Copyright: Pentagon rescue team

77, or even a Boeing 757, remains in doubt. A couple of rivet holes and patterns of parts seem to match with a Boeing 757-200. An engine fragment in the ruins possibly matches with Flight 77's Rolls Royce engine, while another engine part in front of the crash site clearly does not.

Nine/Eleven skeptics say that with so many witnesses including professional photographers around the crime scene the absence

In the ruins lies the diffuser ring of a jet engine compressor. It is said to resemble a Rolls Royce RB211-535E4B, a part belonging to Flight 77, but even if certain elements comply, its true size is hard to judge.[25] On the left is a piece of yellow-primed interior fuselage structure.

Copyright: Pentagon rescue team

Landing gear (presumably the forward unit) was found in the C-ring near the punch-out hole. It looks sturdy enough for an airliner, but the proportions are hard to gauge.

Copyright: Pentagon rescue team

Part of an engine spindle assembly lies on the ground in front of the impact zone. It is far too small to belong to Flight 77's Rolls Royce engine.

Copyright: FEMA

This is what the original Boeing 757's two engines looked like. Copyright: www.rolls-royce.com

Researcher Karl Schwarz traces the engine spindle assembly to this little-known fighter plane. Full story at: http://tinyurl.com/5euu6.

Copyright: Unknown

of clear photographic evidence that Flight 77 hit the Pentagon is in itself suspicious. Supporters of the official story on the other hand generally cite eyewitness testimony.

If there is an absence of clear photos of the plane's impact or debris, and no attempt at all by the Kean Commission to match aircraft parts, the presence of Flight 77 – or at least a Boeing – on the scene is apparently supported by many eyewitnesses. Dozens of eyewitness quotes are to be found on the internet, collated from mostly mainstream media.[26]

Even so, apparently none of the eyewitnesses stuck in the crowded traffic at the time managed to capture a photo of the airliner's extremely unusual flight down the busy Arlington Pike, passing over some ten lanes of morning traffic. Also, it must have looked enormous, but few mention this.

April Gallop was caught in the Pentagon attack. She told investigator Jim Marrs that she was visited in hospital by men who "never identified themselves . . . I know they were not newsmen . . . they told me what to do, which was to take the [compensation] money and shut up. They also kept insisting that a plane hit the building. They repeated this over and over. But I was there and I never saw the plane or even the debris from a plane".[27]

Those who confirm the official story are in a majority, but many are quoted indirectly or in short snatches, and it is not clear that they positively identified a passenger jet. Their number dwindles sharply if you only include those who are unambiguous

Photographer Mark Faram is a senior writer for the *Navy Times*. He told Mentorn films in their September 2004 British TV programme on "9/11 conspiracies" that he saw this aircraft part about ten minutes after the attack and spent another five minutes taking the trouble to "work around to get a shot".[28]

Copyright: Faram/*Navy News.*

Researchers wonder if these men positioned the aircraft part for photographers. One of the (behind) appears to be carrying it. If not, what are they doing? See details at http:tinyurl.com/4uerc

Copyright: Unknown

and do not report impossibilities (like the early reports that the plane hit the lawn).

One witness, seeing the plane from a 14th floor apartment in Pentagon City, said that it "seemed to be able to hold eight or twelve persons" and "made a shrill noise like a fighter plane". Lon Rains, editor at *Space News*, said: "I was convinced it was a missile. It came in so fast it sounded nothing like an airplane." Still another witness, who saw it from his automobile, was reported as saying that it "was like a cruise missile with wings".[29]

But even some of these doubters are convinced their senses have deceived them. It is true that witnesses are influenced by what they are told by figures of authority, e.g. in this case TV newscasters, the Secretary of Defense, or the reporters they speak to, but could so many people all have been hypnotized by authority?

Motorist Penny Elgas, in a traffic jam near the site, said: "At the point where the fuselage hit the wall, it seemed to simply melt into the building." She watched as "the wings disappeared into the Pentagon. And then I saw an explosion and watched the tail of the plane slip into the building."[30]

Major Lincoln Liebner, communications officer for the Secretary of Defense, was on foot "about 100 yards away. You could see through the windows of the aircraft. I saw it hit . . . The plane completely entered the building. I've heard artillery, and that was louder than the loudest has to offer."[31]

USAF Master Sgt Noel Sepulveda, who was in the Pentagon parking lot, said the aircraft had its landing gear down and clipped the light poles (lamp posts): "The plane dipped its nose and crashed into the south-west side of the Pentagon. The right engine hit high, the left engine hit low. For a brief moment, you could see the body of the plane sticking out from the side of the building. Then a ball of fire came from behind it. An explosion followed."[32]

But in the last account, for instance, it is hard to see how a plane the size of the Boeing could have clipped the light poles, dipped down still farther and tilted over without leaving the left-wing somewhere on the lawn.

Pentagon skeptics say witnesses are sincere but as the plane was moving somewhere around 180 metres per second most did not have time to see things clearly and have jumped to conclusions.

So what do the Pentagon skeptics think happened? Some say Flight 77 was shot down and replaced by a drone for practical reasons of manoeuvrability and damage limitation. It is painted in AA livery to trick witnesses who will only see it for a couple of seconds and have no similar previous experience to evaluate the true dimensions of what they are seeing. Many think the drone hit the wall with a missile to enable a clean entry which would explain the lack of debris and reports of an explosion.

Others accept the eyewitness accounts but feel the combination of pilot flying skills, attack path, and low damage warrants the assumption the plane was remote-controlled. Others of course accept the whole of the official story on the Pentagon attacks and simply believe the attacks were allowed to happen.

If it was not the genuine Flight 77, what happened to the passengers? The more radical 9/11 skeptics refer to the Pentagon's Operation Northwoods model. There, the passengers were to be special forces people with false IDs. Some skeptics say that if the Pentagon had a plan to pull off this hoax in the 1960s, the plan should be good for now. Others say the genuine Flight 77 was shot down as was, they suspect, Flight 93.

The silent witnesses, the black boxes that had been stored in the tail of Flight 77, were reportedly discovered in the ruins of the Pentagon "at about 4.00am". The recorders were turned over to the FBI, and then on to the National Transportation Safety Board laboratory in Washington.

A CNN report the same day quoted FBI Director Robert Mueller saying that investigators had recovered "some information" from the flight data recorder. Later, Secretary of Defense Rumsfeld said the data on the cockpit voice data recorder was unrecoverable. Planes have flown at full speed into mountains, been exploded with bombs in the air, and occasionally fallen out of the sky, but this was the first time in forty years of flight recording history that cockpit voice tapes had yielded no information.[33]

7: Flight 93

United Flight 93 left Newark International more than twenty-five minutes late, at 8.42am. The first leg of its flight took it towards Griffiss AFB, the world's most technically advanced Air Force base, bristling with powerful radar, before it turned west.

The Kean Commission Report claims that, after the second aircraft hit the World Trade Center, officials took another twenty minutes to warn Flight 93's pilots of the hijacking danger. This is part of the Commission's portrayal of the FAA as thoroughly incompetent (although no one was subsequently fired).

It was forty-six minutes into the flight when the hijacking is supposed to have occurred, which placed the aircraft within radar range of two US Air Force bases in north-eastern Ohio. Such a long delay in hijacking contrasts with reports that recruits had been trained to attack within ten to fifteen minutes of take-off.[1] The delay occurred on a flight that had already been delayed on the ground by twenty-five minutes. Therefore, one might expect the alleged hijackers to bring their attack forward.

How did the attack work? "All but one of the six passengers seated in the First Class cabin communicated with the ground during the flight, and none mentioned anyone from their cabin having gone into the cockpit before the hijacking. Moreover, it is unlikely that the highly regarded and experienced pilot and co-pilot of Flight 93 would have allowed an observer into the cockpit before or after takeoff who had not obtained the proper permission."[2]

A typical airliner had Airfones fixed to the back of each row of seats. Calls from Flight 93 passed through the Airfone system controlled by GTE.

The Kean Commission continues: "During the first [of two transmissions from the aircraft], the captain or first officer could be heard declaring 'Mayday' amid the sounds of physical struggle in the cockpit. The second radio transmission, thirty-five seconds later, indicated that the fight was continuing. The captain or first officer could be heard shouting: 'Hey get out of here – get out of here – get out of here.'"[3]

Neither of the experienced pilots gave the formal hijacking alerts that would go on record. They were heard shouting "Mayday" over the air at 9.28, but, surprisingly, that did not lead to a hijacking alert. The Kean Commission says: "according to United, the flight's non-response and its turn to the east led the airline to believe by 9.36 that the plane was hijacked" (Kean Commission Report, p. 456 Note 75). So the pilots had not given a hijack alarm, and their cry of "Mayday" had not affected United, even though, "by 9.00, FAA and airline officials [had begun] to comprehend that attackers were going after multiple aircraft," and United had initiated a nationwide ground stop on all its flights at about 9.10, or twenty-six minutes earlier.[4]

Given all these circumstances, skeptics say, it is suspicious that the FAA took another eight minutes to issue the alert: thus conveniently explaining the failure of the military to respond expeditiously.

The Cleveland Airport Mystery

Authorities have given curiously conflicting reasons for why they thought Delta Airlines 1989 was also being hijacked. Virginia Buckingham, in charge of Boston Logan Airport, wrote a year later that: "we received word that a Delta flight out of Logan, bound for the West Coast, had lost radio contact with air traffic control . . . It would be more than an hour before we received word that the flight had landed safely in Cleveland."

But the Kean Commission staff wrote: "Remembering the 'we have some planes' remark, Boston Center had guessed that Delta 1989 might also be hijacked . . . The flight never turned off its transponder. NEADS soon learned that the aircraft was not hijacked." Nevertheless, Cleveland Airport was hastily evacuated when it landed, and Delta 1989's sixty-nine passengers were trapped aboard for two hours as FBI secured the airport and surrounded the aircraft.[5]

In a third account, Transportation Secretary Mineta told the Kean Commission that "Jane Garvey (head of the FAA) had phoned to report that the CEO of Delta Airlines had called the FAA and said it could not yet account for all of its aircraft." So the boss of Delta Airlines put 1989 on the hijack list, while the Kean Commission says it was due to a "guess". Could this have anything to do with confusion over operation Vigilant Guardian?[6]

Meanwhile, at Cleveland, independent 9/11 researchers have dug up a very strange report. The local TV station, WCPO-TV, reported that a mystery flight had landed there: "United identified the plane as Flight 93." Unusually, this report has now been "scrubbed" but researchers have mirrored it and we can confirm having seen it before it was removed as an "error". However, researchers have identified a web of reports, with times, locations, and an interview with a passenger, which all seem to indicate there were two planes at Cleveland, one the Delta 1989 with around sixty passengers, and one the mystery "Flight 93" with around 200 passengers.[7]

Building a Legend and Launching a Slogan

Newsweek and the *Pittsburgh Post-Gazette* were specially briefed with the heroic "Let's roll" cockpit-storming legend of Flight 93. The passengers are depicted storming the cockpit to foil another attack. But the evidence for this depends on one particular inter-pretation of the unreleased cockpit tapes.[8]

The *Newsweek* article was awarded the National Headliner Awards for "Best Coverage of a Major News Event or Topic" for their article. It was headlined "The Real Story of Flight 93" but if any 9/11 skeptics were reading it they were in for a disappoint-ment. Whatever else it was, this was not the sort of investigative journalism that questions the official line.

It is written in a tone of over-the-top emotionalism and propa-ganda, rooting for American faith, righteous pugnacity and revenge, as they describe how "A band of patriots came together to defy death and save a symbol of freedom." It rehearses in full the "ancient litany" (the Lord's Prayer) that football-playing Todd Beamer intoned along with the Airfone telephone supervisor. It lip-curlingly rehearses the instructions included in the terrorist

The Pentagon adopted the "Let's Roll" slogan, shown here on a countdown sign to the anniversary. It was the prime motif of its recruitment campaign for the war in Iraq, making a spurious connection between 9/11 and the oil-rich nation.

Credit: FEMA

handbook that Mohammed Atta had apparently left in his held-back suitcase.

The article recounts: "A thickly accented voice came back on the air: 'Hi, this is the captain. We'd like you all to remain seated. There is a bomb onboard. We are going to turn back to the airport. And they have our demands, so please be quiet.' Investigators think the voice belonged to (hijacker pilot) Jarrah, and that he had flipped the wrong switch, thinking he was addressing the passengers over the PA system when he was calling Cleveland control instead."

There is no evidence that Atta and Jarrah trained together and little evidence they had much contact in the months before the attacks. Addressing and controlling the passengers was an essential part of their plan, so it seems odd that the rogue pilot of Flight 11 made the same error of "flip[ping] the wrong switch", broadcasting to the world the words apparently meant for the passengers.

"After forty seconds of silence, one of the pilots keyed on the microphone again, allowing Cleveland air control to hear more muffled clamor and someone – presumably one of the pilots – frantically shouting, 'Get out of here! Get out of here!' The mike went dead again." It seems odd the pilots did not at this moment press the hijack alarm button that sat right on the control column. If *Newsweek*'s award-winning team asked this question, they certainly provided no answers.

We move on to the passengers. "Todd Beamer may have been having trouble with his credit card, or he may just have punched 0 into the Airfone. In any case, his call at 9.45 was routed to the GTE Customer Center in Oakbrook, Ill." After about fifteen minutes speaking to a total stranger, phone supervisor Lisa Jefferson, we learn that: "Up to this moment Beamer had been all business" – whatever that means.

Then Beamer asks her to promise to call his wife if he doesn't make it home. He tells her about his little boys and the new baby on the way. There is no explanation of why Jefferson did not try to put him through to his wife. It is extraordinary that in a telephone operators' control center a call that was obviously (after the WTC attacks nearly an hour earlier) crucially important was not recorded, either automatically or on Jefferson's initiative. She has since become a minor celebrity and was interviewed for the 2002 Granada TV "docudrama" about the phone calls. In April 2002 Jefferson received a Verizon Excellence Award.

The Kean Commission deals with the array of telephone chatter from Flight 93 by muddying the waters. After stating that the transponder showed Flight 93 was flying at an altitude of about 34,000 feet, it relates that "shortly thereafter, the passengers and flight crew began a series of calls from GTE Airfones and cellular [mobile] phones."

This raises the question we touched on earlier on Flight 77. How could mobiles that A.K. Dewdney could not get working at 8,000 feet get through from four times the altitude, where elementary physics dictates the signal is sixteen times weaker? For months Dewdney, a long-standing contributor to *Scientific American*, was ignored, but by late 2004 mobile phone calls were fast disappearing from the official story.

Skeptics are resigned to never seeing the cellular (mobile) phone billing evidence that could put this troubling matter to rest. Without such evidence, they feel forced to conclude that much of the telephone evidence that supports the storming legend could be just that: pure patriotic propaganda based on mythology. Most reject the possibility of making cellphone (mobile) calls at cruising altitude: they believe most calls must have passed through the GTE system. Some note that using the latest digital techniques, a human voice can be expertly mimicked.

Returning to Flight 93, here is the Kean Commission version of the final minutes:

The hijackers remained at the controls but . . . The airplane headed down; the control wheel was turned hard to the right. The airplane rolled onto its back, and one of the hijackers began shouting "Allah is the greatest. Allah is the greatest." With the sounds of the passenger counter-attack continuing, the aircraft plowed into an empty field in Shanksville, Pennsylvania.[9]

Note here the odd suggestion that passengers continued to beat on the cockpit door while the airliner rolls over and flies upside down. The Flight 93 segment of the Kean Commission Report is written in exactly the same *Boy's Own* adventure story vein as the *Newsweek* report of 3 December 2001.

Ed Felt's last-minute phone call was ignored by the Kean Commission, although there is more hard evidence for it than for the famous Todd Beamer call, which was unrecorded. With the plane by now at low altitude, he was able to use his mobile to dial the emergency number and spoke to phone supervisor Glenn Cramer who told the media: "We got the call about 9.58 this morning from a male passenger stating that he was locked in the bathroom of United Flight 93 traveling from Newark to San Francisco, and they were being hijacked. We confirmed that with him several times and we asked him to repeat what he said. He was very distraught. He said he believed the plane was going down. He did hear some sort of an explosion and saw white smoke coming from the plane, but he didn't know where."[10]

Glenn Cramer was, like air traffic controllers, warned by the FBI not to say any more. The call, which would have been recorded, seems to confirm the jet was shot down or the hijackers had a bomb on board, but it has been airbrushed out of the official story. According to the Kean Commission, the plane crashed at 10.03, discounting the evidence of several seismic stations that the impact occurred at 10.06.

The FBI finally agreed in 2003 to play the cockpit tapes to the victims' relatives. Alice Hoglan was the mother of Mark Bingham who died in the crash. According to CBS: "She said the recording and a transcript the FBI provided to her and other families 'doesn't leave very much doubt at all that passengers were able to get that cockpit door open.' Hoglan said the . . . final spoken words on the recorder seemed to be an inexplicably calm voice in English instructing, 'Pull it up.' She said the English voice toward the end of the recording was so distinct that she believes it's evident the speaker was inside the cockpit."[11]

The calm voice supports a scenario that has been discussed by 9/11 believers in the mainstream US/UK media: the passengers (by coincidence several were big, fit, and combat trained) reclaimed the cockpit and retook the controls at about 9.03 and that the plane was shot down three minutes later in a disastrous error. Nine/Eleven skeptics ask whether there was a shoot down order from plotters to prevent the hijackers being taken alive and spilling out unwelcome information.

Another Aircraft Was There

Flight 93's pilots were warned by United Airlines at 9.23 of the potential for cockpit intrusion and to take precautions and barricade all doors. Whether there was a warning or not, the pilots gave no hijacking alarm before the airliner changed course. The plane turned and flew for thirty-five minutes towards Washington, DC, and the entire array of USAF radar, missiles, and fighter aircraft failed to find it, with most of the passengers reportedly calling friends and relatives during the last twenty minutes of the trip. The plane's transponder apparently went off (or got jammed) at 9.41.[12]

Transponder or not, the absence of a USAF interception, particularly in the wake of the WTC attacks, is remarkable, considering the Air Force's previous record in hundreds of interceptions. Not

Val Mclatchey of Shanksville claimed she took this photograph moments after seeing a fireball rising from beyond the horizon. The FBI reported that an airliner had crashed there. The picture shows that the day was calm, with very little wind. How, then, to explain the debris that was scattered over an eight-mile radius, and the one-ton engine part that lay just over a mile away?

Copyright: Val Mclatchey

A skeptic site reports that the FBI released this photograph "shortly after" the crash. The absence of official vehicles and personnel suggests the timing is accurate. North is at the top. Is this really where Flight 93 crashed? Where is the wreckage?

Copyright: FBI

Environmental officials apparently took this photograph of the crash site, looking from the north-east.

Copyright: Pennsylvania Department of Environmental Protection

FEMA workers and others suppress smoldering embers at the Shanksville, PA, crash site. Something has formed a muddy crater, and the adjoining woods are badly scorched, but there is a peculiar absence of significant airliner debris.

Copyright: FEMA

The A-10 Thunderbolt exactly accords with Susan Mcelwain's description of a plane that appeared with the airliner crash. Skeptics say it might have been there to ensure things stayed to plan, and when they didn't it could have fired the fatal rocket.

one of the Kean Commissioners brought up the sixty-seven Air Force interceptions successfully executed during the year prior to 9/11 (AP, 13 August 2002). The Kean Commission states baldly that there was no attempt at all by the FAA to call in the military, and does not seem to offer any excuse at all. It is almost as if they have simply given up the task by this stage in the narrative.

Skeptics suggest that one explanation for all this would be that the military were already there. Eyewitness statements give a confused picture of the plane's last minutes. But several agree that another plane was present. Some thought it was a business jet, but others made a precise identification of a military fighter plane. Susan Mcelwain, fifty-one, told the *Daily Mirror*:

> The plane I saw was heading right to the point where Flight 93 crashed and must have been there at the very moment it came down. There's no way I imagined this plane – it was so low it was virtually on top of me . . . It had two rear engines, a big fin on the back like a spoiler on the back of a car and with two upright fins at the side.[13]

This is a clear description of a Warthog, or A-10 Thunderbolt (see picture). Was this the aircraft that shot down the rogue airliner? A guided missile would have left a smoke trail and a mid-air explosion that eyewitnesses would remember, and there were a number of eyewitnesses who claimed to have seen Flight 93 explode before it fell to the ground.

After a through investigation, a reporter for the *Independent*, John Carlin, was unable to discount either the shoot down or the bomb explanations. The key part of his story was the one-ton engine part lying 1.2 miles from the crash site. The FBI's explanation that the engine bounced this distance from the impact crater seems next to impossible. This evidence indicates a shoot down rather than a bomb. A heat-seeking missile would shatter the engine, while a small bomb would more likely leave it intact.[14]

Skeptics point out that – much like the other flights – the fate of Flight 93 could be cleared up beyond all doubt by publication of the following evidence, all currently secret. It is hard to see a national security justification for the refusal to divulge the relevant phone records, a map of the whereabouts of collected debris, disclosure of the flight data recorder details, interviews with fighter pilots who were scrambled on the day, interviews with their commanders, and interviews with air traffic controllers. Skeptics of all persuasions can hardly be blamed for observing that these are just the pieces of evidence the authorities refuse to release.

The People

8: The Alleged Hijackers

Let us examine the evidence concerning the alleged hijackers, Al-Qaeda, and Osama bin Laden.

Four days before the US election in 2004 a man identified as Osama bin Laden addressed the world directly on video for the first time since 2001. The figure on the tape admitted responsibility for the 9/11 events. Opinion polls since 2001 showed that whenever a terrorist scare was raised, Bush's approval ratings

2004 US ELECTION

DEC 2001

2001

At first bin Laden made a clear declaration that Al-Qaeda was NOT involved, but his 2001 videos broadcast to the West were ambivalent. After a gap of nearly three years a fuzzy bin Laden video appeared four days before the US elections claiming full responsibility for the attacks. But bin Laden had aged horribly – from kidney disease according to most observers – in the years up to 2001. His appearance now, after three years of supposedly being on the run, was identical. The new bin Laden had not only defied medical science, said many skeptics, but also grown a wider nose in 2001.

went up several points. It is hard to deny the view of many Kerry supporters that in a sense Osama bin Laden won the election for George Bush.

Even some mainstream pundits began to wonder whether bin Laden was rooting for a Bush victory. They noted the argument made by people in the peace movement since 9/11: the logic of war had benefited both Bush and bin Laden. Al-Qaeda had made Bush's presidency with the 9/11 events. Bush had boosted Al-Qaeda in turn by ordering the invasion of Iraq. This had allowed radical Jihaddists to claim the moral high ground. Instead of killing innocent Americans in New York they were now killing the soldiers of a bloody occupation that much of the world regarded as illegal.

The authors of the new video, whoever they were, supported this view, asserting that Al-Qaeda had successfully lured US/UK into a land war against Islam. And in the summer of 2004, one serving CIA analyst even speculated that Al-Qaeda might be planning further attacks on America with the aim of ensuring Bush's re-election.[1]

Among 9/11 skeptics there were varying views. For LIHOP advocates, the video was irrelevant. They concede that bin Laden's people organized the 9/11 events, but think he was unknowingly helped by deliberate White House paralysis of the FBI and FAA. Some MIHOP advocates agreed – they thought that Al-Qaeda had been penetrated by the CIA and the 9/11 plan given inside help.

Others said it would not be difficult to find an actor who looked like OBL and cited the apparently different nose and poor picture quality as evidence the video was a fake. The failure of the new bin Laden to show any ageing was because the tape's authors were trying to make the actor look as similar as possible to existing authenticated pictures.

What about the voice? We are not aware of any publicly independent authentication of the voice, but in any case, as we mentioned in connection with the passengers' phone calls, voice cloning is an announced phenomenon, developed at the Los Alamos National Laboratory.[2]

Prior to the 2004 tape, many observers – including Pakistan's General Musharraf – believed that bin Laden needed kidney dialysis, was extremely weak by the time of his last "official" tape in December 2001, and was probably dead. There was a death notice in the Islamic press.[3] Moreover, *Al-Jazeera* reported that when they interviewed his two top organizers in summer 2002 (see below) they inadvertently referred to OBL in the past tense.

Bin Laden's role was opaque from the start. Late in 2001, at the time of OBL's previous video, there were already strongly conflicting stories about him. In the Urdu language paper *Ummat*, a long-winded bin Laden tells readers: "I had no knowledge of these attacks, nor do I consider the killing of innocent women, children and other humans as an appreciable act." But in an interview with Pakistan's *The Dawn*, a few weeks later, bin Laden – described as healthy-looking, slicker and evasive – claimed a general right to attack Americans. This new, fatter bin Laden appeared again in a questionable video hailed by US/UK as containing a confession, but widely disbelieved elsewhere. The "official" bin Laden video during the same period showed him gaunt and haggard.[4]

In November 2002 a tape was obtained by *Al-Jazeera*, with film of some of the alleged hijackers and supposedly OBL's voice admitting the attacks. Skeptics pointed out that the alleged hijackers could have been filmed by anyone, anywhere. It vanished without trace after French experts questioned the authenticity of the voice.[5]

If the supposed bin Laden videos fail to provide conclusive proof of his authorship of the attacks, the FBI has hardly done any better. There was no paper trail that led back to the caves of Afghanistan. According to FBI Director Robert Mueller: "In our [seven month] investigation, we have not uncovered a single piece of paper – either here in the United States or in the treasure trove of information that has turned up in Afghanistan and elsewhere – that mentioned any aspect of the Sept. 11 plot."[6]

In the following pages we shall see that not only Osama bin Laden but the alleged organizers, the hijackers, and even Al-Qaeda itself, are shrouded in uncertainties over the most basic questions of who they really are and who they were really working for.

The official 9/11 story got a boost, however, when in June 2002 Khalid Sheikh Mohammed (KSM) and Ramzi bin al-Shibh (RBS) – allegedly Al-Qaeda operations chiefs and key 9/11 planners – apparently chose to give an interview while on the run in Karachi to Yosri Fouda of *Al-Jazeera*. Unfortunately the two self-confessed terrorists seized Fouda's video recordings and never returned them, so for the wider world their identities and, therefore, the value of the apparent scoop remained unproven.

Although a 9/11 believer, Fouda has made the odd observation that KSM's "shallow knowledge of both religion and politics caught up with him. He tried to sound authoritative, but he stumbled in his desperate attempts to compose a couple of decent sentences in classical Arabic." This begs the obvious question: if his knowledge of religion and politics was poor, what motivated KSM to organize the attacks at all?[7]

Skeptics also wondered why Al-Qaeda would expose two top operatives to the risk of detection when they could have produced an "official" video in the normal way. Within months Pakistan and the US were announcing the capture of both men, but with contradictory accounts of how, when, and where. Pictures of the men being arrested were never clear, reports of KSM's arrest were denied, and other reports have him dead. The interview with the two men was denounced by an expert cited by the *Financial Times*: "It could have been a script written by the FBI." While a reporter for the *Guardian* wrote: "The story [of KSM's arrest] appears to be almost entirely fictional."[8]

For many skeptics, these two men – apparently talking volubly in custody – far from being living proof of the official story, are prime suspects for CIA-controlled double agents. KSM was also identified by the neocons in Washington as an outsider, their prime suspect for the supposed link man to Saddam Hussein.

Adding weight to the skeptic view, the Kean Commission reports that KSM was working with the Northern Alliance, opponents of the Taliban and Al-Qaeda, and prime beneficiaries of the US invasion of Afghanistan. According to this account KSM changed sides with the express promise from OBL that he would sanction the 9/11 plot.

What about the other co-conspirator, Ramzi bin al-Shibh, apparently a fanatical comrade of Mohammed Atta, based in Hamburg? Here, the Kean Commission accepts the unlikely story that RBS wanted to join the hijackers but failed to get a visa and so restricted himself to back-up work. But why could RBS not have acquired a false ID from the Al-Qaeda passport factory the Kean Commission describes in Afghanistan, for instance, by taking over the identity of a dead Al-Qaeda fighter or a comrade in Germany?

To summarize, the evidence for the involvement of the top two levels of Al-Qaeda (OBL, KSM and RBS) is uncertain: fuzzy videos and confessions made to *Al-Jazeera* or when in US custody. As we have seen, the Kean Commission was given no way to verify these confessions. They were not even allowed to speak to the supposed interrogators.

What about the other two levels – the organizers on the ground, like Mohammed Atta, and the larger group of hijackers that arrived with Saudi passports shortly before the attacks? All 9/11 scenarios come down to the hijackers: were their identities stolen, did they really fly the planes into the buildings (especially the peculiar Pentagon strike), and if so were they helped to success? Could one or more of the organizers on the ground have been double agents, perhaps using a vain, dying bin Laden for their own ends?

In the following pages we will see that far from the certainties of the official story, a confused picture emerges, featuring doubtful identities, radically split personalities, cocaine, possible CIA front companies.

A Question of Identity

Forty-eight hours after the attacks, the FBI published through Associated Press a list of eighteen of the hijackers' identities, basing its list on intelligence information gained from witnesses, electronic flight-manifest logs, and passports reportedly found at two of the crash sites. A short time later they amended the number to nineteen. A few days later, the names were followed with mugshots, obtained from US driving licence and passport authorities. FBI boss Mueller said they were still "determining whether, when these individuals came to the United States, these were their real names or they changed their names . . ."[9]

The *Washington Post* reported: "Saudi Government officials also said yesterday that they have determined that at least two of the terrorists used the names of living, law-abiding Saudi citizens. Other hijackers may have faked their identities as well, they said. 'This operation had tremendous security, and using false names would have been part of it,' said John Martin, retired chief of the Justice Department's internal security section. 'The hijackers themselves may not have known the others' true names.'"[10]

Doubts over identities had been erased from the official story by the time of the Kean Commission. The Kean Commission confirmed that most of the hijackers had obtained new passports prior to the attacks – but then ignored the glaring possibility of identity theft. The Kean Commission claims the US was in most cases unaware of the hijackers before the attacks, and the trail is formed mainly from cash point records, cellphone records (of numbers dialed but not the conversations), flight booking records, credit card records, the occasional report from neighbors and associates (often under suspicion themselves), and internet chat rooms (although few details are given). How could these scant clues rule out the use of false IDs?

The published flight manifests had no Arab names and the numbers of passengers varied, even assuming the hijackers had been deliberately omitted as a matter of policy. A string of corporate media reports said up to seven hijackers were using false IDs, but few mentioned dates of birth or photographs, the crucial details that distinguish people of the same name, thus leaving the stories hopelessly ambiguous.[11]

Newsweek even reported (15 September 2001): "US military sources have given the FBI information that suggests five of the alleged hijackers of the planes that were used in Tuesday's terror attacks received training at secure US Military installations in the 1990s . . . But there are slight discrepancies between the military training records and the official FBI list of suspected hijackers – either in the spellings of their names or with their birth dates."

However, a few reports were clear. The BBC stated that Waleed Al-Shehri had told the media from Morocco that he was still alive: "His photograph was released by the FBI, and has been shown in newspapers and on television around the world. That same Mr Al-Shehri has turned up in Morocco, proving clearly that he was not a member of the suicide attack."[12]

The *Daily Telegraph* reported from Saudi Arabia that "Saudi Airlines pilot, Saeed Al-Ghamdi, twenty-five, and Abdulaziz Al-Omari, an engineer from Riyadh, are furious that the hijackers' 'personal details' – including name, place, date of birth and occupation – matched their own." The paper, quoting an FBI official, offered an explanation that seems highly unlikely in this case: "The identification process has been complicated by the fact that many Arabic family names are similar," and offered an alternative which has been ignored by officialdom ever since: "It is also possible that the hijackers used false identities."[13]

Equally mysteriously, CNN reported this correction: "Based on information from *multiple law enforcement sources* [our italics], CNN reported that Adnan Bukhari and Ameer Bukhari of Vero Beach Florida, were suspected to be two of the pilots who crashed planes into the World Trade Center . . . Federal sources had initially identified the brothers as possible hijackers who had boarded one of the planes that originated in Boston. Their names had been tied to a car found at an airport in Portland, Maine. But Bukhari's attorney said it appeared their identifications were stolen, and said Bukhari had no role in the hijackings." Adnan was alive and Ameer had died in a small plane crash a year earlier. This was presumably the car that was later said to be rented by Mohammed Atta (see below). If so it is hard to see how the two men, Atta and Bukhari, could have been confused in an honest mistake by the FBI.[14]

Even when the autopsy and DNA reports came in, information on the hijackers was scant. The authorities have acknowledged they hold DNA on at least two alleged hijackers' bodies from the WTC, but it would appear that no attempt has been made to match it with any samples held by relatives. Similarly, nothing seems to have been done with baggage apparently belonging to Atta that was seized intact at Boston Airport.[15]

The Kean Commission and the FBI divided the hijackers into the pilot/organizers and the "muscle" who flew in mostly from the Gulf shortly before the attacks. On the pilot hijackers who were in the US for a year or more, there is information from Hamburg, relatives, girlfriends, associates and ordinary Americans who bumped into them.

Most of the "muscle" hijackers arrived with visas issued by the US embassy in Jeddah, Saudi Arabia. J. Michael Springman was the chief of the visa section there in the 1980s. He is a vocal 9/11 skeptic from his experiences in Saudi at a time when the US was backing fundamentalists in Afghanistan: "I issued visas to terrorists recruited by the CIA and its asset, Osama bin Laden," he said later. Springman was fired in the early nineties after making persistent complaints about the irregular visa system.

Springman suspects much the same thing happened in summer 2001, when new regulations made visa processing even slacker. Applicants no longer had to attend in person, he complained. Travel agents "would simply send a package of passports and visa applications over to the Consular's [sic] section. And because they came from a reputable source, people didn't look too closely at it, I guess." This was "an old agency [CIA] ploy".[16]

The *National Review* reported: "According to expert analyses of the visa-application forms . . . all the applicants among the fifteen reviewed should have been denied visas under then-existing law. Six separate experts who analyzed the simple, two-page forms came to the same conclusion . . . *even allowing for human error* [our italics], no more than a handful of the visa applications should have managed to slip through the cracks."[17]

Common sense might dictate that with the applicants no longer present, officials would be more likely to scrutinize the forms and notice that many questions were not even answered. The change in regulations was apparently introduced to reduce the risk of an attack against people queuing outside the embassy.

Who could have been stealing identities and supplying the hijackers? Obviously the first suspect is Al-Qaeda itself, and presumably this is the authorities' unstated reason for ignoring the issue. But, say skeptics, if identities are in doubt, it could have been anybody – from Iraq to the CIA – supplying the hijackers for several different scenarios. A central tenet of the official story is, once again, cast into doubt.

When it comes to studying the principals – Atta, Jarrah and Hanjour – the behaviour in Florida is not at all consistent with any normal sort of Al-Qaeda operative, say the skeptics.

Atta and the Hamburg Cell

It is a central tenet of the official story that Atta was *not* under surveillance in the US and the trail of someone not under close surveillance is limited. While everyone's dialing and billing records are stored by mobile phone companies, it is generally thought the content of calls is not. But the *Knight Ridder* news service reported (6 June 2002) that the NSA was monitoring and translating Atta's calls in the USA.[18]

Moreover, when 9/11 relative and truth campaigner Ellen Breitweiser asked an FBI agent how the Bureau had known exactly which Portland, Maine, ATM machine would turn up a videotape of Mohammed Atta, "The agent got some facts confused, then changed his story."[19]

The *New York Times* (11 November 2001) appeared to confirm that officials had Atta under surveillance: "Mohamed Atta, in seat 8D in First Class, dialed his cell phone for the last time. The call rang . . . on a cell phone belonging to Marwan al-Shehhi, in seat 6C on United Airlines Flight 175. The conversation between the two men, so close that they called each other cousin, lasted less than one minute – just long enough, investigators told *The New York Times*, to signal that the plot was on."

If accurate, these reports put a large question mark over the official story. But a leak in the German media takes the matter farther. German police sources told the mainstream, right of center, news magazine *Focus* (24 September 2001) that they were informed – only after 9/11 – that Atta had been under close surveillance by US "secret service" operatives in Germany in spring 2000, at about the time he was granted his US visa. "It was like all they had to do was push a button" to get information on Atta, said one official, while another said, "It can no longer be ruled out that the Americans kept their eye on Atta after his entry into the United States."[20]

David Edger was CIA station chief in Berlin at the time. In a new role at Oklahoma University in 2002 he explained (according to one report) that "locating terrorist cells, usually consisting of six to twelve members, is the most difficult part of stopping the cell. A member of the cell must turn spy or a person must give a tip . . . Once that happens, taking apart a cell is not very hard."[21]

But Edger is also reported to have told a meeting at the University in 2002, that although officers in Germany knew members of the Atta cell and some of the things they were doing, they had no idea the group would go to different parts of the US, where they would learn to fly planes to crash into the World Trade Center. "In that case, we failed," said Edger.[22]

Intriguingly, Edger was reported in the late nineties to be the CIA's Assistant Director for Operations overseeing clandestine operations throughout the world. Why would Edger suffer an apparent demotion to the Berlin station, and why did his office allow Mohammed Atta to receive a visa to enter the US ask skeptics?[23]

If the Hamburg cell raises embarrassing questions for the CIA it also raises others for the Kean Commission. The Commission goes to great lengths to trace the hijackers' stories, and their main source of evidence is the transcripts of prisoners in US custody and witnesses to the alleged Hamburg Cell. However, they admit they had no access to US-held prisoners. They also had no direct access to the transcripts of their interviews nor, inexplicably, to their interrogators.

There are many reasons why these transcripts could be unreliable or even worthless. The suspects could be informers or agents provocateurs returning to base to help prop up the official 9/11 story, or even imposters, loyal to Al-Qaeda to take the heat off high-level operatives. If on the other hand they are genuine, they could have been tortured or rewarded into confirming the official story. Worse still, say skeptics, they could blurt out information implying the CIA allowed or helped the 9/11 events to happen.

The Kean Commission's other main source on the hijackers is German police interviews with the other "Hamburg cell" suspects, associates of Atta and bin al-Shahib who faced terrorism trials in Germany. Relations with a key ally in the "war on terror", the German Government, were seriously strained in 2004 when the US refused to allow any outside access to KSM and RBS: a refusal that led to the collapse of the case against members of Mohammed Atta's supposed Hamburg terrorist cell.

The reason given to embarrassed German prosecutors and the public for refusing this access and torpedoing one of the few 9/11 trials to take place: the Hamburg terror cell, led by Mohammed Atta and trumpeted for two years as the key to the 9/11 events, in fact never existed.

RBS and KSM had now made statements, supplied by the US State Department, that defendant Abdelghami Mzoudi and Mounir Al-Motassadeq, the latter already serving fifteen years, were never involved in the 9/11 events. This was good news for David Edger – the CIA man in Berlin who conspicuously failed to "take apart" the cell – but from any point of view, it was bad news for justice. Freeing both men, the judge accused America of "trying to manipulate German justice". Prosecutors fumed, saying they still believed the original version.[24]

Living It Up in Florida: Playboys, Drug Dealers or Terrorists?

According to witness reports, the Mohammed Atta who appeared in the US had very different tastes from these modest and obsessively devout student who apparently departed from Hamburg.

The sallow, bitter face of a man known as "Mohammed Atta" appeared all over the US and UK media as that of the ringleader of the attacks. An Egyptian by birth, he had been

Were there two different Ziad Jarrahs? The lips are similar but the head shape and eye color look different. Reports of the key hijackers are so conflicting that 9/11 skeptics suspect identity theft.

Source: FBI

a student for several years in Germany but was registered as a citizen of the United Arab Emirates. According to the witness statements obtained by the German police, Atta was a devout Islamist who led Koranic study sessions.

According to the Kean Commission Report (p. 168), in March 2000, he "emailed thirty-one different US flight schools on behalf of a small group of men from various Arab countries studying in Germany who, while lacking prior training, were interested in learning to fly in the United States". Why would a terrorist openly approach flying schools in the USA in this way? It certainly seems at odds with President Bush's description of Al-Qaeda's methods: "They are sent back to their homes or sent to hide in countries around the world to plot evil and destruction."[25]

If the Hamburg Atta is a committed fundamentalist, the Atta in Florida has a very different lifestyle. When Daniel Hopsicker, a local journalist in Venice, Florida, started to investigate Atta, he discovered a tale of cocaine and alcohol binges, strip clubs, a girl-friend, and a series of witnesses who have been warned by the FBI not to talk:

> An American girl named Amanda Keller, for example, briefly lived with Mohamed Atta in Venice, according to both local news reports and numerous eyewitnesses . . . "They (FBI) told me not to talk to anybody, to keep my mouth shut . . . At first, right after the attack, they told me I must have been mistaken in my identification." Frederickson (a neighbor) stated: "Then they would insinuate that I was lying. Finally they stopped trying to get me to change my story. After that they just stopped by once a week to make sure I hadn't been talking to anyone."[26]

According to Hopsicker, bar manager Tony Amos and bartender Patricia Idrissi – the sources for an early report in the mainstream media on an Atta alcohol binge – later changed their stories and then vanished.

Atta's girlfriend Keller told Hopsicker that when she got a rare look into Atta's personal belongings, she saw multiple IDs issued by various countries sporting very different pictures of "Atta". This character, whoever he really was, was proficient in several languages. As the one-time German defense minister, Andreas von

Huffman Aviation trained some of the alleged hijackers.

Buelow, has argued, the legend of Mohammed Atta is consistent not with an Islamic fanatic but with a double agent, and one of Hopsicker's informants, a former Huffman executive, agrees: "Early on I gleaned that these guys had government protection. They were let into this country for a specific purpose. It was a business deal."[27]

If Atta, reported by Keller to have inexhaustible supplies of cocaine from a nearby airport, had more signs of a professional drug dealer than a religious fanatic, the same applies to the second pilot hijacker, Zaid Jarrah. Jarrah had an active social life and came from a well-to-do family in the Bekaa valley. The notoriety of the Bekaa as the home of Lebanese hashish production has strengthened the view of many 9/11 skeptics that the interest of Atta and Jarrah in learning to fly was somehow linked to the drug trade.

A docudrama on the hijackers was screened on UK TV (Channel 4, 2 September 2004) and focused on Ziad Jarrah and his supposed double personality. The original Jarrah is from a Christian, educated, middle-class Lebanese background – keen on fast cars, drinking, partying, in a long-term relationship with his German girlfriend, Aysel Senguen, the daughter of Turkish immigrants, and planning to get married, when he disappears on 9/11. As the Kean Commossion observes: "Even with the benefit of hindsight, Jarrah hardly seems a likely candidate for becoming an Islamic extremist."

But the Kean Commission – with the help of the German police and their interrogation records – sketches a second, very different personality. "Jarrah Two" (let us call him), is a bearded fundamentalist, receiving training in Afghanistan. But several details of Jarrah Two, downplayed by the Kean Commission and ignored in the docudrama, make the story less plausible. Jarrah's apparently suspicious decision to study aeronautical engineering occurs – not after – but well before he has any contact with Al-Qaeda, and the evil brainwashing is supposed to have started. Moreover, Jarrah's apparent fundamentalism starts to appear not in Hamburg, but after a visit to his secular roots in Lebanon.

According to the Kean Commission, Jarrah Two never made the last sinister phone call from the airport on the morning of 9/11 – the call often cited in the media, and which the docudrama makes its opening scene. It was the normal Jarrah: "in the early morning hours of September 11, Jarrah made one final call to Senguen from his hotel . . . The conversation was brief and, according to Senguen, not unusual."[28]

Senguen has also denied that a letter from Jarrah, seized by the FBI after it was apparently wrongly addressed, constitutes the confession that the media claimed. She says that oblique references taken to refer to the 9/11 plot were simply about the upcoming wedding and his decision to defy his family and take flying lessons, a dream since childhood. The *LA Times* reported that Jarrah didn't go to prayers, had no connection with Atta in Hamburg, and that his flight school comrades completely disbelieved the allegation he was a hijacker.[29]

One of the oddest aspects of the official hijacker narrative is the large number of unnecessary plane flights they made, particularly Jarrah who also made hundreds of phone calls to his girlfriend. For those outside the law, any airport is an extremely hostile environment, a choke point where you and your luggage can be examined in great detail. IDs are checked and matched against any new information, photos taken covertly. Of course, these systems often fail, but with the hijackers safely in the US, why take the risk?

If there is any truth in the official story of Jarrah, then he was an infiltrator recruited in Lebanon (with or without his family's knowledge) to penetrate Al-Qaeda via the militant Hamburg mosques, and set up with aeronautical skills to make him more attractive as a recruit. He never intended to die and was either duped into sacrificing his life in the attacks or is still living, under a new identity. For LIHOP skeptics, Jarrah is simply a schizoid, highly unreliable operator, one more example of how such an amateurish plot needed inside help to succeed.

After an extensive investigation, CNN had this exclusive on 1/8/2002: "[Jarrah] was stopped and questioned in the United Arab Emirates in January 2001 at the request of the CIA, nearly nine months before the attacks, sources in the government of the UAE, and other Middle Eastern and European sources told CNN. The CIA wanted him questioned because of 'his suspected involvement in terrorist activities,' UAE sources said."[30]

The Kean Commission reports the stop, but without any mention of a CIA role. If the "multiple sources" who confirmed this are right, then here is powerful new evidence that, whether he was a genuine terrorist, a victim of identity theft, or an infiltrator, the CIA knew about yet another suspected hijacker before the event.[31]

Most Elusive Plane Had Most Elusive Pilot

As we have seen, Flight 77 was, from the start, the plane that 9/11 skeptics focused on. Internet activist Brian Quig, famous for his allegations of CIA drug running and later to die in an apparent car accident, put it like this: "[when Flight 77] bypassed a straight in shot at the offices of the joint chiefs of staff only to hit an insignificant spot in the back of the Pentagon. I said to myself then, it is not a real terrorist attack!"

Hani Hanjour, named by the Kean Commission as the pilot, must have been a natural in the cockpit to make the official story work. Early reports had him making an "irrecoverable" dive, but the physical evidence contradicted this. Hanjour must have made a ground-hugging approach characteristic (as Dulles flight controllers expressed it) of military aircraft.[32]

The BBC's Tom Carver dug up yet another Flight 77 coincidence. The alleged hijackers "succeeded because they lived and worked, not in the shadows where spies operate, but in full view. In fact, one of the most bizarre ironies of all this is that five of the hijackers lived in a motel right outside the gates of the NSA. Early on the morning of September 11, when Hani Hanjour and his four accomplices left the Valencia Motel on US route 1 on their way to Washington's Dulles airport, they joined the stream of NSA employees heading to work."[33]

"Hani Hanjour" (left at cash point pictured with Majed Moqed) was supposed to be the pilot who attacked the Pentagon.

Source: FBI

Just who was Hani Hanjour? The Kean Commission's details on Hanjour are even sketchier than those on the other ringleaders: he is a trained pilot with a private licence issued in 1996, and most surprisingly – in view of what happened later – an FAA commercial certificate, issued in April 1999. A report in the *Washington Post* added intriguingly that how and where he received this licence "remains a lingering question that FAA officials refuse to discuss".[34]

The *Washington Post* also describes Hanjour in 1998, training hopelessly on a simulator in Phoenix, and quotes instructor Wes Fults as saying: "He had only the barest understanding what the instruments were there to do." Around January 2001, the Kean Commission reports, a similar Hanjour, shows up in the US and, after a "refresher course", trains on Boeing 737 simulators at the Pan Am flight school in Mesa Arizona. He is advised to give up by his instructors, but persists and finishes initial training only at the end of March. In June 2001 Hanjour tries to fly down the Hudson corridor as a trainee but the instructor is so unnerved by his lack of skill that he refuses a second run.[35]

Nine/Eleven skeptics are doubly suspicious of a report buried in the Kean's Commission's footnotes: a Hanjour with far greater skill reappears dramatically in August 2001: "Hanjour successfully conducted a challenging certification flight supervised by an instructor at Congressional Air Charters of Gaithersburg,

Maryland, landing at a small airport with a difficult approach. The instructor thought Hanjour may have had training from a military pilot because he used a terrain recognition system for navigation."[36]

For some 9/11 MIHOP skeptics there is an explanation for all this: the real Hanjour – described as weak, timid, and hopelessly incompetent – never got a commercial license. It was a forgery. An imposter was used to persuade the Maryland school of his skills, in particular the ground-level flying so necessary for the Pentagon attack that Hanjour was scripted for.

Hijackers were supposedly caught passing through security at Dulles International Airport in video footage released in mid-2004. Compare this unidentified video frame with the one depicting Atta at Portland, which has proper identifiying data.

Copyright: AP

Mohammed Atta and the Lost Luggage

We have seen that there are inconsistencies in the official portrait of the hijackers. One crucial incident seems to strengthen the skeptic case farther. Atta's visit to Portland Airport on the morning of the 9/11 events, is, as the Kean Commission agrees, inexplicable. It also concerns a crucial part of the evidence that helped establish the official story in the media: the photos of Atta and Al-Oman together in different locations and Atta's incriminating baggage that somehow missed the Flight 11 connection.

Atta took a connecting flight from Portland to Boston on the morning of that day. But no one can explain why he would take such a flight when he was already in Boston the day before. A car parked at Boston Logan Airport was traced to an Atta accomplice. Why did Atta and his partner hire another car, drive from Boston to Portland the evening before, and take a connecting flight back from Portland to Boston at 6.00am next morning? The Kean Commission says it is a mystery, while admitting it is one that the FBI did not investigate in its enormously painstaking and expensive PENTTBOM Inquiry.[37]

Atta's motivation must have been intense, because by taking a connecting flight on the same day as the planned attacks, he was imperilling the whole scheme, of which he was ostensibly the leader. If for some reason the Portland

"Atta" (behind) and "Al-Omari" obligingly got both their faces into one shot for the surveillance camera at a cash machine in Portland, Maine, at 8.56pm on 10 September 2001. They had driven there from Boston to take an inexplicable connecting flight back first thing in the morning.

Source: FBI Link

Here, the men called Atta and Al-Omari are video-grabbed at Portland, Maine, Airport, supposedly on their way to Boston Logan Airport to hijack American Airlines Flight 11. Strangely, they were at Boston the previous day.

Copyright: Portland Police

flight were badly delayed or even cancelled, he would be unable to make the crucial first and most damaging strike on the North Tower of the World Trade Center. If he failed to use his cellphone to call his Boston accomplices on Flight 175 at Logan, as they sat on the apron, they might cry off.

The photos taken by surveillance cameras at Portland Airport were flashed round the world and gave a kick start to the official story in the vital first hours after the attacks. Few realized that the photos of Atta and Al-Omari were taken at Portland, not Logan, which apparently did not have surveillance cameras.

Was this the motive for the alleged hijackers to take their mysterious connecting flight? Did they want to put their photos and baggage on record as a discreet admission of guilt from Al-Qaeda? Suppose they suspected there were no checkpoint surveillance cameras at Logan. It might give them a reason to travel via an airport that had them. Perhaps the bags, too, were the motive but the the Portland flight could not have been a way deliberately to reveal the incriminating contents of his luggage, unless Atta had an accomplice in baggage at Logan. However, the Kean Commission makes no mention of any investigation of baggage handling in the FBI's PENT-TBOM investigation.

We have to ask: how could Atta know there were no surveillance cameras at Logan?

ICTS, one of the two know companies with the contract to provide security at Logan, was hardly likely to disclose such information to inquiring Islamists. And even if we accept that Atta somehow found out, perhaps by diligently reading the security trade press or searching deeply on the internet, the question still remains: how could he have manipulated the baggage hold-back?

The hold-back itself is something of a mystery. When he checked in at Logan, Atta's name reportedly triggered the security computer (CAPPS), which meant that "his checked bags were held off the plane until it was confirmed that he had boarded the aircraft" (Kean Commission Report, p. 1). This cannot be quite right, since the baggage never made it onto the plane.

The salient point about the bags held back at Logan is that they immediately confirmed the official story of Arab hijackers. It could not have been a deliberate admission of Al-Qaeda guilt, because Atta would have needed an accomplice in baggage handling, an obvious implication that was never investigated. Atta was ostensibly on a suicide mission: he needed no baggage. This "mystery" as the Kean Commission calls it, is resolved for skeptics by the blatantly incriminating nature of the otherwise useless baggage contents: a handheld flight computer, flight simulator manuals, two videotapes about Boeing aircraft, a slide rule flight calculator, a copy of the Koran, airline uniforms (in some reports), an Arabic suicide attacker's handbook written in Islamic rhetoric, and the owner's last will and testament. Short of a confession in English or a bag of drugs this could hardly be a more suspicious collection of luggage, why risk taking it on the journey?

The uniforms, useless in any Al-Qaeda plan (because they were out of Atta's control in the luggage system) and posing an obvious extra risk, would, however, make plenty of sense if anyone was engineering events from the US side. Did someone wish to give a hint about how the otherwise inexplicable hijackings had been executed? The failure of any of the eight airline pilots to give a hijack warning remains a central mystery of the attacks. Could someone have foreseen this problem and packed uniforms to feed the media a believable narrative about clever, deceptive Arab fanatics who bluffed their way into the cockpits as visiting crew?

A former high-level intelligence official told the famous US investigative journalist Seymour Hersh: "Whatever trail was left was left deliberately for the FBI to chase." (*New Yorker*, 1/10/01) But one clue on the trail was overlooked. If it was a subtle admission of Al-Qaeda responsibility, why did he risk everything by taking the connecting flight with this incriminatory luggage at all?

The skeptics have an alternative scenario: the connecting flight had to be made so that Atta could be photographed and the bags could be opened, thereby incriminating Arabs. Only inside operatives could be certain of making that happen, so either Atta was not genuine or he was manipulated by them.

But the oddities do not end there. Atta apparently threw a FedEx bill into a trash can at the Comfort Inn in Portland, Maine, which is supposed to have led investigators to an Al-Qaeda account in Dubai, United Arab Emirates, allowing them to claim they had tracked down the funding for 9/11 (*Newsweek*, 11/11/01, *London Times*, 12/1/01). Was this an act of carelessness, was Atta already under surveillance, or was this a trail left deliberately?

Al-Qaeda: Friend or Foe?

In these pages we examine the role of Al-Qaeda outside the 9/11 events, with a view to gleaning information that might cast more light on them. This can also serve to check the official 9/11 narrative, two central tenets of which are that the US had no information from within Al-Qaeda and that it is an evil enemy. We will see that both are misleading. In some theatres, Al-Qaeda seems to have been in the role of ally. In addition, other recent Al-Qaeda attacks have aroused suspicions of collusion.

As we have seen in the intelligence world, there are always likely to be large gray areas of double agents, alliances with third parties, infiltration by other agencies, "turned" captured operatives, and so on. Here are two examples where the US received human intelligence on Al-Qaeda which was then ignored:

A long-time FBI source and his case officer were ignored in April 2001, and when they went to the Kean Commission were ignored again. Here is the worldnetdaily version of what they then told the media: "the long-time FBI source is said to have told two counter-terrorism agents from the Washington field office that Al-Qaeda planned to carry out terrorist attacks in major US cities, including New York, using planes and suicide operatives. The two agents took the tip seriously because the asset . . . had Afghan contacts close to Al-Qaeda's inner circle."[38]

Local TV in Florida reported that Randy Glass, a private US citizen working as an undercover agent in a government sting operation, learned about a threat to the World Trade Center from Pakistani ISI agents. He tried to warn various officials in government before 9/11. Florida State Senator Ron Klein and US Senator Bob Graham admit being given a warning.[39]

Even in the case of the aborted 1993 WTC attack by Ramzi Yousef, there was evidence of a gray area. Emad Salem, had helped with the making of the bomb. But Salem had taped his discussions with his FBI handler, which suggested FBI involvement in building the bomb. In one passage, Salem says in broken English: "It was built by supervising supervision from the Bureau and the DA and we was all informed about it and we know what the bomb start to be built. By who? By your confidential informant. What a wonderful great case!" Rather than denying this accusation, the FBI officer's reply is: "No, don't make any rash decisions. I'm just trying to be as honest with you as I can."[40]

Somehow, a plan to supply harmless powder was aborted in the FBI and instead the bomb attack went off as planned. As the

New York Times put it with characteristic understatement: "The account . . . portrays the authorities as being in a far better position than previously known to foil the 26 February bombing of New York City's tallest towers." Robert I. Friedman, investigative reporter for New York's the *Village Voice*, reported his Israeli intelligence sources as saying Ahmad Ajaj – another WTC bomb plotter – was an agent for Mossad.[41]

The complicated and treacherous reality of the world of Al-Qaeda, the ISI, and the CIA, was underlined in Afghanistan in 2001, when, during the US-backed invasion, planeloads of privileged Pakistani, Taliban, and Al-Qaeda fighters and leaders were flown out of Kunduz where they were trapped. The foot soldiers were left to a horrible fate, with many killed in atrocities.[42]

Made in the USA

The evidence suggests there is no clear-cut separation between Western governments and Al-Qaeda. Bin Laden's anarchic structures offered shelter to self-professed Jihadists – who could just as easily have been infiltrators, agents provocateurs, simple murderers, or heroin dealers. This is the ideal environment to carry out a LIHOP or MIHOP plot. This ambivalent side to Al-Qaeda has been there from the beginning.

The Al-Qaeda story starts in the late 1970s. As Zbigniew Brzezinski, national security advisor to the then President Carter, has described, the Soviet Union was consciously lured into Afghanistan as a strategic ploy to involve them in a long, Vietnam-type guerrilla war. An alliance was formed between the Christian West and the Muslim East against atheistic communism. America's allies in the Muslim world were fundamentalist Wahabi Muslim Saudi Arabia, and the brutal machiavellian Pakistani intelligence agency, the ISI, which grew during the long Afghan struggle into a major power in the land.[43]

The massive support from America was channeled through the ISI, so Osama bin Laden – in his support office in Peshawar – was able to say later that he did not know where the money was coming from. This seems unlikely, but the relevance for us is that bin Laden operated with the blessing of the ISI, who later allowed him to return to Afghanistan, controlled in 1996 by their close allies the Taliban. Here are three cases that indicate Al-Qaeda was linked with US/UK during the 1990s:

Al-Qaeda and MI6 worked together on a plot to murder Libya's Ghadaffi.

Anas Al-Liby, the man MI6 allegedly paid, is now listed as captured and described as an Al-Qaeda training camp commander.

Source: FBI

■ A plot by Britain's MI6 to murder Libya's Colonel Ghadaffi, while still denied by the UK Government, has been confirmed by renegade Secret Intelligence Service (MI6) officer Richard Tomlinson, and became the center of the Shayler affair. David Shayler alleged that MI6 officers planned to pay £100,000 to Libyan Jihaddist Anas Al-Liby, who was already a bin Laden lieutenant. Later, Al-Liby was on the US Government's most wanted list with a reward of $25 million for his capture for his involvement in the African embassy bombings. Al-Liby reportedly lived unmolested in the UK until he managed to escape a police raid and flee the country in May 2000. *USA Today* (2/3/2002) has listed him as captured and described him as an Al-Qaeda training camp commander.[44]

■ *Guardian*, 22 April 2002: "The official Dutch inquiry into the 1995 Srebrenica massacre, released last week, contains one of the most sensational reports on Western intelligence ever published. Officials have been staggered by its findings . . . Now we have the full story of the secret alliance between the Pentagon and radical Islamist groups from the Middle East, designed to assist the Bosnian Muslims . . . a vast secret conduit of weapons smuggling though Croatia . . . was arranged by the clandestine agencies of the US, Turkey, and Iran, together with a range of radical Islamist groups, including Afghan Mojaheddin and the pro-Iranian Hizbullah . . ." A mysterious fleet of black C-130 Hercules aircraft probably run by the Pentagon helped fly Mojaheddin fighters in.

■ The *Independent*, 21 October 2001: "Interpol believes that Osama bin Laden is linked to Albanian gangs who have taken over a growing web of crime across Europe. The investigations into organized crime links with his terrorist network also show that Mr bin Laden supplied one of his top military commanders for an elite KLA unit during the Kosovo conflict. Gwen McClure of the criminal subdivision of Interpol revealed the Albanian connection in a briefing to the cross-party NATO parliamentary group of MPs."

After 9/11: the Gray Area

Some suspect that even after 9/11 nothing much has changed. Al-Qaeda, if not controlled by the outside agencies, is, with its devolved structure and necessarily fluid personnel, vulnerable to manipulation. Each apparent Al-Qaeda operation should be evaluated separately, say the skeptics.[45] Here are some examples of events they are suspicious of:

■ The 2004 Madrid bombings led to the unexpected fall of the pro-Bush Aznar Government. The explosives were supplied to the presumed Al-Qaeda cell by a Spanish group with links to the police. When officers raided Suárez Trashorras, the Spanish man who had allegedly supplied the explosives, they reportedly found by chance, on a piece of paper in his wife's possession, the home telephone number for a senior bomb squad officer. The plot thickened when the Spanish daily *El Mundo* claimed that three men suspected of stealing the explosives from a local mine had worked "before and after" with police in Northern Spain.[46]

■ In the Philippines skeptics became highly suspicious when local newspapers reported in July 2002 that CIA-linked US national was found in The Evergreen Hotel, Davao City, on the island of Mindano, after a bomb blast in his room. At the time, an alleged Al-Qaeda bombing campaign was being used to justify a security clampdown involving joint US Filipino anti-terrorist actions. The US national was reportedly spirited out of the country by US security officials even while facing potential terrorism charges.[47]

■ Although this affair was ignored in the mainstream media, it had major repercussions for the US. Naomi Klein reported in *The Nation* that a large group of soldiers, led by a Lieutenant Antonio Trillanes, mutinied, accusing the Philippines Government and senior military officials of responsibility for the series of bombings that had led to the massive US presence there. The US presence was rapidly wound down.[48]

Osama's Lucky Escapes

Intelligence agencies may have to work on the basis that "the devil you know is better than the devil you don't know". With patience, a terrorist organization can be infiltrated, influenced, perhaps even controlled. We have seen that there is some support for the allegation from many 9/11 skeptics that this is what has happened to Al-Qaeda. Here we look at the evidence of bin Laden's lucky escapes.

For skeptics, the evidence that OBL was protected at times by the US is clear. There would be a range of possible motives for this, but they all add up to one proposition: the US felt OBL was more use to them free than captured. This would imply, in turn, that they had some sort of influence, if not control over Al-Qaeda and with it a major part of radical Islam. The most likely means for this is an agent in the leadership.

For 9/11 believers, on the other hand, the fundamentalist rhetoric of good and evil that has been lavishly applied to Al-Qaeda leaves little room for doubt. The failure to capture OBL can only be seen as misfortune, bad communications, or perhaps incompetence. The Kean Commission devotes much space to this issue. But the report restricts itself to a tedious discussion of the CIA's attempts to capture or kill OBL in the three years immediately before 9/11.

Madeline Albright: the government of Sudan offered the Clinton administration a dossier on bin Laden, they refused to look at it.

Sudan 1995 is the scene of bin Laden's first lucky escape. Keen to find favour with the international community, the Sudanese Government handed over for trial in France, Carlos "the jackal" – the notorious Venezuelan pro-Palestinian terrorist. But when they approached the US embassy with a full dossier on bin Laden and his "terrorism incorporated", to their astonishment, the US would not accept it, reported David Rose in *Vanity Fair*. Timothy Carney, the US ambassador at the time, told Rose that Washington "lost access to a mine of material on bin Laden and his organization."[49]

Bin Laden, with a lavish contingent of equipment and camp followers – more reminiscent of a medieval court than a terrorist on the run – eventually proceeded to Afghanistan. When this issue was raised shortly after 9/11, the White House passed up an opportunity to reaffirm their theme that Clinton had been soft on terrorism. Instead, National Security Advisor Condoleezza Rice made the unlikely claim that the ambassador's recollections were simply wrong.

Many 9/11 skeptics say this report is a smoking gun. The mainstream French conservative newspaper, *Le Figaro*, reported that bin Laden spent ten days from 4 to 14 July 2001 in the American Hospital in Dubai under Dr Terry Calloway, receiving kidney treatment. At this time, OBL was on the FBI's most wanted list and blamed for the attack on the USS *Cole* and bloody truck bombs against US embassies in Kenya and Tanzania. The paper said that among his many well-connected visitors were relatives from Saudi and the local CIA station chief, who was recalled to Washington the day

Le Figaro reported that bin Laden had hospital treatment in Dubai, where he met the CIA station chief.

after bin Laden went. *Le Figaro* quotes an unnamed senior hospital administrator, while Calloway refused to comment.[50]

According to Dan Rather of CBS, bin Laden was back in hospital, one day before the 9/11 events. On 10 September, this time, courtesy of America's ally Pakistan. Sources in Pakistan's ISI told CBS that bin Laden had received dialysis treatment in Rawalpindi, and hospital workers confirmed the claim. Perhaps realizing the very serious implications, Dan credited the report to "one of the best foreign correspondents in the business, CBS's Barry Petersen".[51]

Tucked away in the print section of the *Observer* was news of another lucky escape, this time from a US bombing raid in Afghanistan. Bin Laden's entourage apparently received news which decided them to quit a farm hours earlier than planned. Shortly after they left the farm was the target of a US raid.[52]

The last credible sighting of bin Laden in 2001 had him vanishing into the fortified Tora Bora cave complex near the border with Pakistan. With the area surrounded, there seemed no escape for bin Laden. But the US chose to rely on Afghan mercenaries to cut off the final escape route to Pakistan. Bin Laden seems to have escaped again: the consensus is that he paid his way past the mercenaries. There is no obvious explanation why the US did not deploy their own troops.[53]

The left-wing US website Counterpunch, run by Alexander Cockburn, interviewed Kabir Mohabbat, an Afghani exile from Houston, Texas, who had been retained by the US State Department in the last months of the Clinton presidency to negotiate with the Taliban for the handover of bin Laden. Mohabbat reports the Taliban were only too willing to get rid of OBL, who they regarded as a liability. A plan was agreed between the Taliban and US representatives in Frankfurt in November 2000: OBL would be put under house arrest and his compound would be hit by a cruise missile.

But the plan was put on hold pending the new presidency. The new team sent several messages to the Taliban during 2001, each asking for more time to take a final decision. If Mohabbat is to be believed, the same extraordinary paralysis that we find in other areas was also affecting this offer from the Taliban. In an echo of its treatment of whistleblower Sibel Edmonds, the Kean Commission has no reference to Mohabbat's testimony, reports Counterpunch: "he told his story to the 9/11 Commission (whose main concern, he tells us, was that he not divulge his testimony to anyone else), also to the 9/11 Families who were pursuing a lawsuit based on the assumption of US intelligence blunders by the FBI and CIA. He says his statements were not much use to the families since his judgment was, and still remains, that it was not intelligence failures that allowed the 9/11 events, but criminal negligence by the Bush administration."[54]

9: Paralysis at the FBI

"All appropriate action was taken based on the threat information we had," Ari Fleischer told CBS News in May 2002. "The president did not – not – receive information about the use of airplanes as missiles by suicide bombers."

However, in 2004 the famous August 2001 memo from the CIA to President Bush was forced into the public domain by pressure on the Kean Commission from suspicious relatives of the 9/11 victims. It showed that denials like this might have been literally true, but they were disingenuous. The President had been warned that Al-Qaeda was planning to strike in the US and that it might hijack aircraft.[1]

In any case, for many skeptics the more relevant issue was what the CIA knew. Its dedicated bin Laden unit – with its knowledge of Al-Qaeda intentions and methods – had received warnings from different quarters. Foreign leaders passed on urgent warnings from their own agencies and FBI agents on the ground had reported suspicions from more than one field office. After 9/11 the CIA told the world – mostly through journalists in anonymous leaks – that they had had no human intelligence on

Al-Qaeda: but in the previous chapter we have seen two instances that contradict this.

The issue of ignored warnings is relevant to what we have called "Step 2", necessary in any 9/11 plot: the paralyzing of the government machine by top officials. The warnings raise two questions: why weren't they acted on? And how could officials like Rice, Cheney, or Blair have claimed they were taken completely by surprise when the attacks came?

Clearly there is a great deal of room here for the incompetence theory: mistakes are made and, as is routine in politics, blame is shifted. This political need to shift the blame could explain why the post-9/11 official estimates of Al-Qaeda's strengths are now generally recognized to be massively overstated.

Skeptics who have examined the political and governmental paper trail have found there is a story of multiple warnings, a lack of response to them, and a general White House posture in its diplomatic activities in 2001 that simply doesn't seem to add up.

In these pages we look at the warnings, the peculiar response to them, the whistleblowers in the FBI, and the activities of the White House in the months leading up to the 9/11 events. We start by looking at five of the warnings from foreign leaders. These were a long way from the mere "intelligence chatter" that officials imply is all they had to go on. Most imply personal decisions by very busy people to repeat messages their officials would already have given the CIA.

"US and Italian officials were warned in July that Islamic terrorists might attempt to kill President Bush and other leaders by crashing an airliner into the Genoa summit of industrialized nations, officials said Wednesday . . . Italian officials took the reports seriously enough to prompt extraordinary precautions during the July summit of the Group of 8 nations, including closing the airspace over Genoa and stationing antiaircraft guns at the city's airport . . ." *Los Angeles Times*, 27 September 2001.

In the case of Russia, Putin told MSNBC just after the attacks, he had ordered Bush be warned "in the strongest possible terms" of an impending attack. According to a story in *Izvestia* on 12 September, which has since been partially removed from their website, Russian intelligence warned that, based on tape-recorded conversations of suspects, up to twenty-five terrorists (including two Uzbeks on forged passports) and pilots were training for missions within the US.

From Germany, it was reported the ambassador himself had warned top US officials on the basis of information from German intelligence (BND) surveillance of what was to become the "Hamburg cell". According to the conservative German daily,[2] *Frankfurter Algemeine Zeitung*, the BND warned both the CIA and Israel in June that Middle Eastern terrorists were "planning to hijack commercial aircraft to use as weapons to attack important symbols of American and Israeli culture".[3]

Even if the US did not, as they claimed, have any intelligence directly from Al-Qaeda, a correspondent from the Arab satellite station MBC reported in June 2001, after a meeting with bin Laden: "A severe blow is expected against US and Israeli interests worldwide . . . There is a major state of mobilization among the Osama bin Laden forces."[4]

The most spectacular claims came from Israel. In leaks, officials claimed that Mossad, their secret service, had passed on actual names. According to the *Daily Telegraph* (16 September 2001), two senior Mossad experts were sent to Washington in August 2001 to alert the CIA and FBI. The list they provided supposedly included the names of four of the 9/11 hijackers. Globe-Intel, run by Gordon Thomas, a freelance correspondent for the *Daily Express* (London), added a claim – sourced to Mossad – that they had infiltrated the hijackers.[5]

All Quiet At FBI Headquarters

With warnings flooding into the White House and the CIA in July 2001, the reaction of officials was bordering on the perverse. Richard Clarke, the long-standing White House anti-terrorism co-ordinator, who had been moved from the National Security Council to the Deputies Committee by Rice, said later that he and CIA boss George Tenet had their "hair on fire". But he testified that despite his best efforts, Rice and Ashcroft had been uninterested in terrorism prior to the 9/11 events. The Kean Commission agreed they had taken months even to hold the first official strategy meeting.[6]

Can the "failures" of summer 2001 reasonably be explained by lack of interest or even incompetence from top White House officials? We now know that contrary to statements at the time, officials had been warned that the attacks, like the failed millennium attack, were likely to occur in the US. On 12 July 2001, Assistant FBI Director Dale Watson, chief of the counter-terrorism division, told the National Governors Association that "[We are] headed for an incident inside the United States." This was confirmed when the President's 6 August 2001 memo was released by the Kean Commission, its title: "Osama bin Laden Determined To Strike in US".[7]

The lead agency in the US mainland for counter-terrorism was the FBI, because the CIA was banned from its inception from operations at home. What was going on at the FBI? According to the President's memo, drawn up by the CIA and presented personally by Tenet at Bush's Texas ranch: "The FBI is conducting approximately seventy full field investigations throughout the US that it considers bin Laden-related."

However, the President was being seriously misinformed. FBI spokesman Ed Coggswell told the media during the Kean

Commission hearings in 2004 that they were "trying to ascertain how the number seventy got into the report. Those investigations involved a number of international terrorist organizations, not just Al-Qaeda." Many were criminal investigations, unlikely to focus on preventing terrorist acts. He would "not characterize the targets of the investigations as cells, or groups acting in concert, as was the case with the Sept. 11 hijackers".[8]

Rice explained to the Kean Commission there was no paper trail to show the White House had responded to the July flap because they hadn't needed to. FBI headquarters had already "tasked all fifty-six of its US field offices to increase surveillance of known suspected terrorists" and to contact informants who might provide leads.

But this was also inaccurate. Here is Kean Commission member Roemer: "We have done thousands of interviews here at the 9/11 Commission. We've gone through literally millions of pieces of paper. To date, we have found nobody – nobody – at the FBI who knows anything about a tasking of field offices. Nothing went down the chain to the FBI field offices . . ."[9]

So just what was going on at the FBI? Their ultimate boss, Attorney General John Ashcroft, told the US Senate on 9 May 2001 that his number one priority was to protect the American people against terrorism. But the Kean Commission discovered a 10 May Justice Department document setting priorities for 2002. There was no mention of counter-terrorism. Thomas Pickard, acting FBI director in the summer of 2001, told Kean he had briefed Ashcroft on terrorist threats in late June and July 2001 but the Commission quoted Pickard as saying: "After two such briefings, the attorney general told him he did not want to hear this information anymore."[10]

FBI Agents Are Blocked, Threatened

FBI headquarters officials told the 2002 Congressional investigation into 9/11 that they had "failed to join the dots" (9/11 skeptics were amused at this choice of words, as for them it describes precisely the mistake 9/11 believers make). Overworked officials weren't quite vigilant enough. Perhaps they felt that instead of looking for a needle in a haystack they would wait for tip-offs. As Richard Clarke put it: "Now, in retrospect, we now know that there was information in the FBI that hadn't bubbled to the top."

But, say skeptics, officials failed to join just two dots: one, the warnings from the CIA and the White House and two, the very urgent messages from a series of their own agents in the field who were, astonishingly, being blocked by their superiors from conducting urgent Al-Qaeda investigations of hot suspects. The details, say skeptics, indicate very strongly that this was not a passive failure but an active one: one that cannot be explained by incompetence.

In addition to the warnings from abroad there were domestic warnings which should have reached Ashcroft through two channels. David Shippers sent a warning that FBI agents were having their very urgent Al-Qaeda investigations obstructed by officials at FBI headquarters. Shippers' name should have made officials take notice: Shippers was a Republican hero, the lead counsel in the impeachment of President Clinton in 1999. Shippers also passed warnings to a range of Congressmen and women.

Nafeez Mosaddeq Ahmed collated Shippers' allegations in his seminal book on 9/11, *The War on Freedom*: "According to Shippers, these agents knew, months before the September 11 attacks, the names of the hijackers, the targets of their attacks, the proposed dates, and the sources of their funding, along with other information. At least two weeks prior to September 11, the FBI agents again confirmed that an attack on lower Manhattan, orchestrated by Osama bin Laden, was imminent. However, the FBI command cut short their investigations . . . threatening the agents with prosecution . . ."[11]

In the months after 9/11, Shippers' allegations were corroborated by whistleblowers from the FBI. Headquarters had received urgent messages from its own officers, and in brazen contrast to what top officials were telling the President, it was blocking their investigations. Yet the Kean Commission failed to address the concerns of these crucial whistleblowers in its final report – people who had made headlines at the time of the Congressional Inquiry in 2002. The Commission's readers, if they shared his short memory span, were left with the erroneous impression that information might indeed have simply "failed to bubble up".

In 10 July 2001 in what came to be known as the Phoenix memo, agent Ken Williams warned of an "effort by Osama bin Laden to send students to the US to attend civil aviation universities and colleges" and suggesting a national database be set up of suspicious trainee pilots. His request was ignored.[12]

In January 2005 evidence emerged to support David Shippers allegations of even more specific foreknowledge within the FBI. A US court found that Jeffrey Royer, described as a former FBI man, was convicted of feeding classified information to Anthony Elgindy, a stock trader. Both were convicted of racketeering and securities fraud. The BBC reported "One of the more bizarre aspects of the trial focused on the claims that Mr Elgindy may have had foreknowledge of the 11 September terrorist attacks in New York and Washington. Mr Elgindy had been trying to sell stock prior to the attack and had predicted a slump in the market. No charges were brought in relation to these allegations".

FBI agent Robert Wright of the Chicago field office, who had been investigating a suspected terrorist cell for three years, was informed in January 2001 that the case was being closed. Three months before September 11, Wright wrote a stinging internal memo charging that the FBI was not interested in thwarting a terrorist attack, but rather "was merely gathering intelligence so they would know who to arrest when a terrorist attack occurred". According to one report, Wright has gone so far as to accuse the FBI of "intentionally thwarting investigations of known terrorists".[13]

In January 2005 evidence emerged to support David Shippers allegations of even more specific foreknowledge within the FBI. A US court found that Jeffrey Royer described as a former FBI man was convicted of feeding classified information to Anthony Elgindy, a stock trader. Both were convicted of racketeering and securities fraud. The BBC reported "One of the more bizarre aspects of the trial focused on the claims that Mr Elgindy may have had foreknowledge of the 11 September terrorist attacks in New York and Washington. Mr Elgindy had been trying to sell stock prior to the attack and had predicted a slump in the market. No charges were brought in relation to these allegations".[14]

On 28 August 2001 the New York FBI office tried to open a criminal investigation into alleged hijacker Khalid Almihdhar, based on evidence he had been involved in the USS *Cole* bombing. Their requests for information were turned down, although there was a considerable interest in him in the CIA. The Kean Commission reported that key evidence was withheld from the New York FBI agents by an agent named "Jane" on the grounds that it was intelligence and had to be kept separate from the criminal process.[15]

This separation at the FBI is known as The Wall. As applied in the summer of 2001 it meant that most of the FBI agents investigating Al-Qaeda crimes and potential crimes were officially starved of information from the CIA or any other agency on the other side of The Wall, such as the vital National Security Agency, which seems to have been intercepting some of the hijackers' communications. Official regulations ensured that the FBI, the only agency with a chance of stopping 9/11, was refused help.

In the case of Almihdhar, the block was not legal. The Kean Commission states: "'Jane' sent an email to the [New York FBI] agent explaining that . . . the case could be opened only as an intelligence matter, and that if Mihdhar was found, only designated intelligence agents could conduct or even be present at any interview. She appears to have misunderstood the complex rules that could apply to this situation." He gives two clear reasons why Jane was wrong.

How could "Jane" have made this critical "misunderstanding", working against her fellow FBI agents and as it turned out missing a crucial chance to thwart the 9/11 events? In the footnotes, the Kean Commission concedes that "Jane" had already had the rules explained to her by FBI lawyers. Moreover, when "Jane" sent the vital email to the New York agent she failed to copy it to the legal supervisor, who would have pointed out her mistake.[16]

Nine/Eleven skeptics say those on the CIA side of The Wall went out of their way to torpedo the investigations of FBI field officers. For them, The Wall is the legal smokescreen used by the plotters to paralyze the FBI and the "Jane" memo, an example of the block in action. The key legal memos that created The Wall, and put US mainland counter-terrorism in the hands of a select Washington coterie of CIA officers, were written in 1995. Coincidentally, the author of the memos was none other than Kean Commission member Jamie Gorelick, who wrote them when she was a Justice Department official under Clinton.

Minnesota Memo: the Smoking Gun?

Step in Coleen M. Rowley, FBI Special Agent and Minneapolis Chief Division Counsel. Rowley was not just an experienced FBI special agent, one of the first female FBI agents to be appointed following legendary FBI boss J. Edgar Hoover's virtual ban on women agents, but a lawyer too. In an angry May 2002 memo, she detailed precisely how FBI headquarters had spiked the Minneapolis investigation into suspected twentieth hijacker Zacarias Moussaoui, and it involved much more than incompetence and omission.[17]

Moussaoui had been arrested for overstaying his visa following a tip-off from a flight school that he might be a terrorist intending to hijack aircraft, and agents wanted a search warrant to examine his laptop computer.[18]

The unnamed headquarters supervisor whose permission was needed to apply for the warrant refused to forward the request to the Department of Justice, saying there was a lack of "probable cause" – the case was too weak. But Rowley's team contacted the French

FBI agent Coleen Rowley blew the whistle on the FBI block.
Source: Steve Wewerka, *New York Times*

authorities who confirmed that Moussaoui was, in their opinion, a dangerous terrorist and a member of Al-Qaeda. In Rowley's words:

> While reasonable minds may differ as to whether probable cause existed prior to receipt of the French intelligence information, it was certainly established after that point and became even greater with successive, more detailed information from the French and other intelligence sources.

This was not a casually taken position by FBI HQ, the long wrangle became very detailed. For instance, the Paris telephone directory was consulted to show that contrary to the assertions of HQ, Moussaoui was not a common name in France and had been correctly identified.[19]

As Rowley put it: "The fact is that key FBI HQ personnel . . . continued to, almost inexplicably, throw up roadblocks and undermine Minneapolis's by-now desperate efforts to obtain a FISA search warrant . . . HQ personnel brought up almost ridiculous questions in their apparent efforts to undermine the probable cause. In all of their conversations and correspondence, HQ personnel never disclosed to the Minneapolis agents that the Phoenix Division had, only approximately three weeks earlier, warned of Al-Qaeda operatives in flight schools seeking flight training for terrorist purposes!"

In desperation, Rowley's office contacted the CIA's Counter-Terrorist Center (which incidentally had a staff of around thirty exclusively on the bin Laden case, a key team that is barely mentioned in the Kean Commission). They were "chastised" for this by FBI HQ. But the CIA had a very different view of the Moussaoui case. The Kean Commission discovered that "George Tenet and his deputies at the Central Intelligence Agency were presented in August 2001 with a briefing paper labeled 'Islamic Extremist Learns to Fly' about the arrest days earlier of Zacarias Moussaoui, but did not act on the information."[20]

So information FBI HQ was telling Rowley did not justify an application for a search warrant was featured in a briefing to the CIA Director! As if this were not enough, Rowley complained that FBI HQ had left out key information which they had promised her they would include, weakening her case. She added pointedly: "the Supervisor's taking of the time to read each word of the information submitted by Minneapolis and then substitute his own choice of wording belies to some extent the notion that he was too busy."

On a superficial reading, the presumption in Rowley's memo is that the official 9/11 story is true. But the memo is sprinkled with information like this which implies that it cannot be the whole truth, and that FBI HQ is "circling the waggons". After September 11, in FBI offices and even HQ, she records that:

> almost everyone's first question was "Why?" – Why would an FBI agent(s) deliberately sabotage a case? (I know I shouldn't be flippant about this, but jokes were actually made that the key FBI HQ personnel had to be spies or moles, like Robert Hansen, who were actually working for Osama bin Laden to have so undercut Minneapolis's effort.) Our best real guess, however, is that, in most cases avoidance of all "unnecessary" actions/decisions by FBI HQ managers (and maybe to some extent field managers as well) has, in recent years, been seen as the safest FBI career course.

But this was not a case of playing safe. The official's position was in defiance of everything that was supposed to be going on in Washington at the time: Tenet with his hair on fire, the "tasking" of FBI field offices.

Is Rowley, a legally trained long-term career officer, really being flippant here or is she going as far as she dare to blow the whistle on what she suspects but cannot prove: that a part of FBI HQ was actively colluding in the 9/11 plot? If she had gone any further would anyone have believed her anyway? The only practical strategy for a whistleblower who suspects the worst is to say what they are sure of, and hope someone will step forward to provide the next piece of the jigsaw. So far in the 9/11 case the process has worked well, say skeptics – but painfully slowly.

Rowley provides one more piece of evidence, which, if anything, is even harder to square with the official story. On September 11 the FBI officers made yet another attempt to open Moussaoui's laptop. Rowley describes FBI HQ's response when, even with the towers crumbling, they still refuse to act on Moussaoui: "this was probably all just a coincidence and we were to do nothing in Minneapolis until we got their (HQ's) permission because we might 'screw up' something else going on elsewhere in the country."

This points to the only possible legal explanation for obstruction of justice at FBI HQ: that there was another, better investigation into the hijackers which FBI field offices might "screw up" if they were allowed to interfere. Let's call it Operation X. The problem is that this elephant in the sitting room has vanished without trace. Rowley's memo is all but ignored by the Kean Inquiry.

Operation X was similarly invisible to the earlier Congressional Inquiry, which was given an inaccurate portrayal of the Moussaoui case by officials from FBI HQ. When Rowley's memo was published it elicited this reaction from Senate Judiciary committee member John Edwards: "Based upon that briefing [by the FBI], I actually felt reassured about the vigor with which the Moussaoui investigation had been conducted," but "There are some things that have come to light since that time that I was not told about."[21]

One thing is certain: the mystery operation failed. So why was it completely invisible to the Congressional Inquiry and the Kean Commission? Two possibilities arise, say skeptics. Firstly, skeptics suggest, the inquiries have colluded in a massive cover-up of what really went wrong. Perhaps they were told the operation was still ongoing and had to be kept secret for reasons of national security. Or, secondly, the justification for the FBI block could not stand any examination, and the officials involved made sure Operation X was covered up from investigators.

Either way, 9/11 skeptics see much the same scenario. Operation X, run by the small X Team, serves to paralyze enforcement activities so that the FBI and everyone else on the wrong side of The Wall is prevented from intervening, even when faced with a case like Moussaoui. They say that for LIHOP, Operation X could simply be a surveillance operation against the hijackers, a surveillance that is doomed to fail. For MIHOP "X" is a more active operation lending at least a degree of help to the hijackers, or even stealing identities for a more fraudulent scenario.

Was "X" a secret annex to George Tenet's plan drawn up in 1999 to combat Al-Qaeda, known across government, according to the Kean Commission, simply as "The Plan"? Or was it run from the White House and the Pentagon with Tenet and Clarke out of the loop? Skeptics believe that with the right powers of subpoena and the right body running a criminal inquiry, a handful of senior FBI and CIA officials should be able to clear the matter up.

In a sad postscript, Rowley – who had been made a person of the year by *Time* magazine in 2002 and had even been put forward for a senior Headquarters role – announced her resignation from the FBI in January 2005. Although the FBI had kept its public promise not to punish her for her memo, she was demoted in 2003 after expressing fears that the war in Iraq could lead to an increase in terrorism.[22]

10: Line of Deceit

In 2003 Michael Meacher – until that spring, Labour's longest serving front bench MP – wrote a bombshell article for the *Guardian* entitled, "This War on Terrorism is Bogus":

The Project for the New American Century (PNAC) plan shows Bush's Cabinet intended to take military control of the Gulf region whether or not Saddam Hussein was in power. It says "while the unresolved conflict with Iraq provides the immediate justification, the need for a substantial American force presence in the Gulf transcends the issue of the regime of Saddam Hussein."

The so-called "war on terrorism" is being used largely as bogus cover for achieving wider US strategic geopolitical objectives . . . plans for military action against Afghanistan and Iraq were in hand well before 9/11 . . . could US air security operations have been deliberately stood down on September 11? If so, why, and on whose authority? The overriding motivation for this political smokescreen is that . . . by 2010 the Muslim world will control as much as 60 per cent of the world's oil production and, even more importantly, 95 per cent of remaining global oil export capacity.[1]

As an experienced politician, Meacher was aware of another aspect of the case. The *cui bono?* (who benefits?) approach has been used since the days of Rome to disentangle conspiracies and assassinations.

This political argument for LIHOP has three legs: one, the attacks helped to realize existing US plans; two, the attacks were necessary for these plans; three, the plans required the attacks just at the time they occurred. After Meacher's original article appeared, both critics of the White House and the Kean Commission (in its limited inquiries into White House decision-making) delivered a considerable amount of evidence to support the LIHOP thesis. This book is primarily concerned with the direct evidence on 9/11, but this political evidence for LIHOP is compelling. In the following pages we sketch out the series of events and policy developments at the Bush White House in the order they occurred, a sequence that has led many politically literate citizens to suspect the worst.

In 1989 the Cold War ends with the collapse of the Berlin Wall, the peace movement calls for massive cuts in the US military industrial complex. US strategists rethink policies. Military spending falls. Hawks start searching for new enemies.

Oil takes center stage in 1991 as Saddam Hussein is evicted from Kuwait. According to Indian Foreign Minister at the time, Inder K. Gujral, US Secretary of State James Baker "minced no words when he told me: 'Mr Minister, oil is our civilization and we will never permit any demon to sit over it.'"[2]

Throughout the 1990s US/UK maintain rigorous sanctions, some say genocidal sanctions, on Iraq, causing major problems in the UN and with global public opinion. In the US, pressure from the network we now know as the neocons makes for the Iraq Liberation Act, signed into law by Clinton in 1998. Regime change is now official US policy.

By 1997 the Taliban have taken over most of Afghanistan. Texas oil barons see them as a good thing, offering the security needed for a gas pipeline from Central Asia down to a partly Enron-owned plant in India. In 1997 the Taliban are feted on a visit to pipeline company Unocal in Texas.[3]

In 1998 the spectacular and destructive African embassy bombings put Al-Qaeda high on the US agenda. CIA boss George Tenet comes up with a new 1999 plan to combat Al-Qaeda. The Kean Commission says this was universally known as "The Plan", but the plan as reported by the Kean Commission has little new. Nine/Eleven skeptics suspect there is a top-secret extra element in it.

The destroyer USS *Cole* is badly damaged in a suicide attack in Yemen in October 2000. The Kean Commission confirms the Clinton administration sees Al-Qaeda as a top problem. White House aides meet twice weekly. In an unprecedented move, the incoming Bush administration leaves all the top anti-terrorism officials in place, including CIA boss George Tenet and Richard Clarke, as national anti-terrorism coordinator in the White House.

January 2001, Treasury secretary Paul O'Neill confirms later that Iraq is top of the Principals' agenda from day one of the new presidency.[4] White House anti-terrorism chief Clarke is downgraded from the Principals Committee to the Deputies Committee. The first time the Principals discuss Al-Qaeda is one week before the attacks. A State Department envoy reports in 2004 that the Taliban are offering to hand over bin Laden, but the White House refuses to make a decision.

Spring 2001, Rumsfeld explains eloquently to the Kean Commission that there is no support in the US for an invasion of Afghanistan to deal with the Al-Qaeda problem and no preparations made. But Rumsfeld's testimony is contradicted by the President. Bush told the Kean Commission he had "concluded that the United States must use ground forces for a job like this", and is quoted another time as saying, "I'm tired of playing defense. I want to play offense. I want to take the fight to the terrorists." An unnamed White House official tells Reuters (5/8/2002): "Our strategy became focused on eliminating Al-Qaeda, not trying to 'roll it back'."

Summer 2001, the US policy stance is: another attack is inevitable, something must be done, nothing can be done, a land war against the Taliban is the President's preferred solution. Wolfowitz opines that the USS *Cole* attack is politically "stale". This points to one simple solution, say skeptics – wait for the next attack and use it as a reason to invade Afghanistan. As it happens, by June 2001, the system is, as the Kean Commission quotes, "blinking red" with terrorist warnings. Ashcroft has apparently been warned not to travel on commercial flights – but he denies this. Meanwhile, he tells FBI officials that "he did not want to hear" about reports of an increased risk of terrorist activity (Ashcroft has denied this claim, made under oath to the Kean Commission by acting FBI Director Tom Pickard).

"**Summer 2001**, to borrow a phrase from Sherlock Holmes, sees "the dog that didn't bark in night." Skeptics ask why, just a few months after the *Cole* attack, neocons who are looking for an excuse to hit Afghanistan and Iraq do not make political capital out of the terrorists' threats as the system blinks red. Why not start the public campaign that will be needed for the military plans? Nine/Eleven skeptics have an explanation: the A Team depend on paralysis of the defenses, their plot could be wrecked if a propaganda drive led to a widespread improvement in security.

Mid-July 2001, reports circulate that the Taliban will award the pipeline project to Argentine consortium Bridas and not to America's Unocal. State Department officials are openly threatening an attack on Afghanistan in diplomatic meetings in July. Pakistani diplomat Niaz Naik told the BBC's George Armey US diplomats said there would be an invasion if bin Laden was not handed over. The invasion would take place in October before the weather changed. How could US diplomats be so sure they would be invading Afghanistan within three months?[5]

July 2001, Cheney is currently in charge of not only the top-secret "energy taskforce" but also a national taskforce on "preparations for managing a possible attack by weapons of mass destruction and more general problems of national preparedness". The taskforce has no officially recorded meetings prior to 9/11. The official announcement as cited by Kean was no longer on the White House website when we checked late in 2004.[6]

July 2001, at the Genoa summit, surrounded by anti-aircraft batteries, as a result of an inexplicit terrorist threat, a protestor from the seemingly unstoppable global justice movement is killed by Italian police. In South Africa, Colin Powell, subject to heckling for US support for Israel, walks out of the UN Conference on Racism. The US has never been so unpopular.

August 2001, Tenet presents Bush with "August memo", warning of Al-Qaeda intent to attack America and hijack planes. The President is reassured by the ongoing FBI investigations into this, but the Kean Commission decides Tenet's information is wrong. It emerges later that the inacurrate information was omitted from a parallel briefing to second-tier officials.

August 2001, Tenet tells Kean in unambiguous terms that he had no farther meetings with the President in August, but has to apologize for misleading the Commission when the CIA HQ puts out a statement contradicting this. Tenet had traveled to Texas for a special meeting on 24 August. Bush remarked the next day: "We got back here at about 11.30am and met until 5.15pm I think they left. That's the longest meeting I've had in a long time, on a very important subject."[7] What did this meeting discuss, asks skeptics?

1–10 September, eighty federal officials raid the offices of Infocom in Texas, which hosts hundreds of Arab and Islamic websites, including *Al-Jazeera*: the media sector best placed to challenge the official story is out of action.[8]

10 September, Enron is about to go belly up. As a long-time friend of CEO "Kenny Boy" Lay and massive recipient of Enron campaign funds, Bush is vulnerable. The media recount of the Florida vote is pending and reporters have discovered thousands of mostly black voters were wrongly struck off the voting register. The economy is heading for a violent recession. None of this has reached the public, but Bush is already low in the polls.

10 September (abroad), there is a consensus among world leaders that the Bush regime, having blocked the Kyoto accords on global warming and undermined other treaties, is excessively isolationist. Nine/Eleven will be seen as a splendid opportunity to show America support and encourage it to confront the problems of the outside world, especially by leaders with their own "terrorism" problems, like Aznar, Putin, and Sharon.

September 11, in the words of the *Washington Post*'s Bob Woodward, is the defining moment of the Bush presidency.[9] Blair probably reacts faster than the Pentagon to the attacks. Within minutes he has abandoned a speech to the TUC conference and rushes to London, within hours he had phoned key foreign leaders.[10] By that evening major leaders are singing from the same song sheet.

The Senator and the General

Two days before the 9/11 events, the *Karachi News* suspected something big was going to happen:

> ISI Chief Lt-Gen Mahmud's week-long presence in Washington has triggered speculation about the agenda of his mysterious meetings at the Pentagon and National Security Council . . . What added interest to his visit is the history of such visits. Last time Ziauddin Butt, Mahmud's predecessor, was here during Nawaz Sharif's Government

the domestic politics turned topsy-turvy within days. That this is not the first visit by Mahmud in the last three months shows the urgency of the ongoing parleys.

On the morning of September 11, 2001 Florida Senator Bob Graham, chairman of the Senate intelligence committee, was in a meeting with General Ahmad. A few weeks later Ahmad resigned and disappeared from public life after press stories linked him with the Al-Qaeda funding chain.

"US investigators believe they have found the 'smoking gun' linking Osama bin Laden to the September 11 terrorist attacks, with the discovery of financial evidence showing money transfers . . . The man at the center of the financial web is believed to be Sheikh Saeed, also known as Mustafa Mohamed Ahmad," declared the *Guardian* on 1 October 2001. The full name was Ahmad Omar Saeed Sheikh, a British national, and like many senior Al-Qaeda people, something of a middle-class jetsetter.[11]

Maria Ressa of CNN (6 October 2001), based in New Delhi, took it further: "investigators have now determined that Ahmed Umar Syed Sheikh and Mustafa Muhammad Ahmad [the name used to transfer the Al-Qaeda money] are the same person, it provides another key link to bin Laden as the mastermind of the overall plot." Two days later, she referred to "Ahmed Umar Syed Sheikh, whom authorities say used a pseudonym to wire $100,000 to suspected hijacker Mohammad Atta". ABC's chief investigative reporter, Brian Ross, told viewers (30 September 2001): "federal authorities have told ABC News they've now tracked more than $100,000 from banks in Pakistan to . . . suspected hijack ringleader Mohamed Atta."

There should not have been much doubt over this identification of Ahmed Umar Syed Sheikh and Mustafa Muhammad Ahmad, because *Newsweek* reported (11 November 2001) that the FBI had video footage of the latter at a bank in the UAE.[12]

But a bombshell came on 9 October from *The Times of India*: "The US authorities sought [General Ahmad's] removal after confirming the fact that $100,000 were wired to WTC hijacker Mohammed Atta from Pakistan by Ahmad Umar Sheikh at the instance of General Mahmud. Senior government sources have confirmed that India contributed significantly to establishing the link between the money transfer and the role played by the dismissed ISI chief . . . including Ahmad Umar Sheikh's mobile phone number, [which] helped the FBI in tracing and establishing the link."[13]

No evidence of the General's role in the transfer of money has been seen. But to skeptics it seems astonishing that the US would simply accept the resignation of someone they thought had financed the hijackers and gone on to make fools of everyone that mattered in Washington as he lingered in high-level discussions for a week after the attacks. It should also have been a massive worry that with Pakistan nuclear armed, General Mahmud, as one of the most powerful figures in the land, would have had little trouble obtaining nuclear materials for Al-Qaeda.

If Ahmad was involved as alleged in the article only pressing for his resignation suggested to the skeptics that this was not the response to an enemy but to someone who has been caught out and needs to keep a low profile. If Pakistan posed a real risk, they say, why did the US invade Afghanistan with only 10,000 men and move straight on to Iraq? For 9/11 skeptics, Ahmad is a likely linkman between the CIA and Al-Qaeda.

Asia Times reported (8/4/2004) that "Tenet and Deputy Secretary of State Richard Armitage had been in Islamabad in May, when Tenet had 'unusually long' meetings with Musharraf. Armitage for his part has countless friends in the Pakistani military and the ISI."

Skeptics see more support in what happened next. General Ahmad vanished from public view and the media went silent on the money trail, eventually asserting (AP, 18 December 2001) that the person behind the Mustafa Ahmad alias was not Sheikh Saeed but a new character altogether: Sa'd al-Sharif, an in-law of bin Laden. When the *Wall Street Journal*'s Daniel Pearl went to Pakistan to investigate this he wound up dead.

Senator Bob Graham, on the other hand, established a name for himself as a Bush critic. By 2004 in his book, *Intelligence Matters*, he was blaming Al-Qaeda sympathizers in Saudi Arabia for complicity in the attacks.

The Amerithrax Affair

An American public already stunned by the 9/11 events was shocked to learn only three weeks later that a terrorist was sending letters tainted with anthrax. The letters were all branded with the 9/11 date, although the liberal targets of the letters seemed more appropriate for a right-wing fanatic than a hate-filled Arab.

After a photo editor, Robert Stevens, died from inhaling anthrax at *The Sun* tabloid newspaper building in Florida, four more deaths followed from letters containing anthrax that were sent to media outlets, including newscaster Tom Brokaw and the Capitol Hill offices of Senators Tom Daschle, D-S.D., and Patrick Leahy, D-Vt. Postal facilities closed, as did office buildings on

This is the anthrax-bearing letter sent to House Democratic leader Tom Daschle. The message is clearly headed 09-11-01, although it was sent weeks after that date. Some people think "Allah is great" is not an authentic-sounding invocation. The writer apparently left no DNA or fingerprints, and the letter was later decontaminated by irradiation.

Capitol Hill, where hundreds of lawmakers, staff members and others were tested and given an antibiotic. At the Brentwood facility, two postal workers died from inhaling anthrax.

This was manna for the "Iraq Liberation" lobby in Washington. Who but Saddam could have supplied Arab terrorists with anthrax, they asked? Nine/Eleven skeptics were thrown into despair. Here was an obvious follow-up operation to boost the official 9/11 story, distract attention from any doubts, frame Iraq, and terrorize the Democrat opposition, they felt. It looked to many like the second stage of a coup. As the eminent law professor Francis Boyle put it:

> Clearly this was a deliberate attack designed to shut down Congress, the House and the Senate, which they pretty much did, at a critical time. And it was by people affiliated with Pentagon, CIA. I do not believe that at all was any coincidence.[14]

But then spores were identified by scientists as a particular strain, stemming only from the government's own labs at Fort Detrick, Maryland. The media agreed it was probably the work of domestic criminals. The attempt, nearly successful, to frame Iraq was quietly abandoned. The neocons instead concentrated on the report, later discredited, that Mohammed Atta had met an Iraqi agent at Prague Airport. The anthrax investigations went onto the back burner.[15]

In the judgment of Barbara Hatch Rosenberg, from the Federation of American Scientists, the culprit was "part of a clique that includes high-level former USAMRIID scientists and high-level former FBI officials. Some of these people may wish to conceal any suspicions they may have about the identity of the perpetrator, in order to protect programs and sensitive information. This group very likely agreed with David Franz, former Commander of USAMRIID, when he said 'I think a lot of good has come from it. From a biological or a medical standpoint, we've now five people who have died, but we've put about $6 billion in our budget into defending against bio terrorism.'"[16]

The Corporate Media: Preachers of the 9/11 Religion

When we spoke to a leading figure in the UK legal establishment about the 9/11 events, he was intrigued to hear what the alternative scenarios might be, but said he could not, of course, believe any of it. This was for the very good reason (in his mind) that "the media would have found out" if the official version had been wrong.

Much information has indeed come out. This book has assembled many reports from the media that raise suspicion. In the memorable expression the FBI used to explain their "failings" over 9/11, many have noticed these reports, "joined the dots" and become 9/11 skeptics. Several of these skeptics, like Gore Vidal and Michael Meacher, have a public platform in the media and have used it.

Nonetheless, the continued assumption amongst editors and reporters is that the official story of 9/11 is true. This belief requires not just a rebuttal, but a convincing explanation, from all 9/11 skeptics. This book has tried to set out the counter-arguments of 9/11 skeptics without making an overall judgment. However, we are clear on one thing: to broadcast the official story of 9/11 as certain truth is to misrepresent the evidence that has been presented, and to ignore the surprising absence of evidence that should have been presented. We offer an explanation for how the media could have got it so wrong.

There is a parallel with the Iraq WMD scandal, when false information was presented to the public not as allegation but as fact. Then, too, information was available that revealed the official line to be questionable: for instance, from experts like ex-arms inspector Scott Ritter, but they were tucked away in reports that were subsequently ignored by editors – who hold the real power in most publications.

This hazy video-grab taken from the roof of the Palestine Hotel, where many mass-media personnel lodged during the Baghdad walk-over, proves that the Saddam statue-wrecking event was staged by US Army psy-ops experts. The jubilant crowd the media reported applauding the liberators is actually the small group of hand-picked Iraqis on the right performing for Coalition's assembled cameras. The square is secured against other Iraqis by US tanks and troop patrols. Credit: Information Clearing House

When challenged over what many considered at the time to be falsehoods, reporters would say the allegations had been proved, or simply that everybody knew they were true, while politicians in US/UK suggested dissidents were fools or even supporters of the enemy. In both 9/11 and Iraq the evidence – such as it was – was supplied and controlled by the intelligence services.

Newsgathering is like the process of osmosis. *Facts* are sucked into the system like nutrients into a plant, but then they are filtered through structures determined by media owners – if they are not compatible with the structure they don't get any farther. (Many of these "facts" are in any case merely statements by politicians making unproven – and as we saw in Iraq – even wholly false assertions.)

The basic unit of journalism is not the "fact", it's the structure it fits into: the *story*. As the newsroom cynics say: "don't let the facts

The *London Evening Standard* used this photograph on its front page next day, showing what had magically changed into a crowd of hundreds cheering the Americans on.

Credit: memoryhole.com

Jessica Lynch became an icon of the US-led Iraq invasion. When coalition forces were bogged down, with hopes of a quick victory apparently receding, her story blitzed the news media with US heroism. The story "will go down as one of the most stunning pieces of news management yet conceived", wrote the *Guardian* (15 May 2003). As the BBC later revealed in an authoritative documentary presented by John Kampfner, the entire Lynch legend was a fabrication from beginning to end. Lynch had not been wounded in battle, but in a mundane road accident. She had not been held captive by the Iraqi enemy, but cared for in a civilian hospital by staff who gave her transfusions of their own blood. Iraqi doctors had actually attempted to return her in an ambulance but been turned back at a US checkpoint. Nor had she been rescued by intrepid US forces battling with heavily armed insurgents. The hospital had been undefended. Nor was Lynch happy about her stardom: she was extremely upset about being used for hysterical and misleading media hype by the Pentagon and its friends in the US corporate TV media. Skeptics wonder whether the US corporate war machine similarly rigged the events of 9/11 and the media coverage in order to manipulate public opinion against Arabs and in favour of the attack on Iraq.

get in the way of a good story." The story is heavily influenced by the editor, who takes orders indirectly from the media owner. The editor also knows that a story will run more convincingly if it draws from, and adds to, the current *narrative*. After 9/11 the narrative was particularly clear – Orwellian slogans like "America under attack" were on the news screens for weeks on end.

In the wake of 9/11, the mass media enthusiastically fostered a climate of flag-waving patriotism. They conflated Iraq's dictator with Osama bin Laden, until many Americans believed Saddam Hussein, and not bin Laden, had organized and recruited the reputed hijackers. TV channels fog-horned the administration's terrifying warnings about Iraq's weapons of mass destruction (WMD), until the US public was prepared to accept claims such as the one uttered by the President in a televised address on 17 March 2003: "The Iraq regime continues to possess and conceal some of the most lethal weapons ever devised."

In fact, Israel had flattened Iraq's single nuclear reactor at Osirak before it was completed, in a bombing raid in 1981. United Nations weapons inspectors later prevented the deranged dictator from getting anywhere near building the Bomb. His drone missiles looked more like converted lawn-mowers. But the national delusion was so complete, that when the truth was finally recognized in mid-2004, the *New York Times* was worried its war-mongering had fatally damaged its reputation as a journal of record. It published an unprecedented apology for misleading the public.[17]

The *Washington Post* followed suit and ladled out heaps of remorse for its abysmal coverage of Iraq's alleged WMD. But after providing the reader with a 3,000-word article detailing the months of shoddy reporting and war-mongering hype (including scores of misleading headlines), the *Post* still shrugged its shoulders and denied any responsibility for causing the war. The apologies seemed to be more of a cynical PR move than anything else.[18]

Other individuals gave belated and cautious mea culpas, such as ITN's Nick Robinson who wrote (*The Times*, 16 July 2004) that he could "see why [his] reporting angered those who opposed the war", but "It was my job to report what those in power were doing or thinking . . . That is all someone in my sort of job can do. We are not investigative reporters . . . Now, more than ever before, I will pause before relaying what those in power say. Now, more than ever, I will try to examine the contradictory case."

Robinson confesses: "It was my job to report what those in power were doing or thinking . . . That is all someone in my sort of job can do . . ." But he misses the meat of the issue. The point is that he, like many journalists, reported the unproven allegations they were making with the implication that these allegations were fact.

Robinson suggests they could not have done anything else. But why could reporters not have referred to "Iraq's *alleged* weapons of mass destruction" – particularly in the build-up to invasion, when UN inspectors had visited the alleged weapons sites and found them empty? Why could they not have applied the same standards to the Prime Minister as they would apply to anyone else? Why could they not look at the politicians' track record of honesty and truthfulness, and evaluate their current statements in this light? Journalists pride themselves on their skepticism. Cannot Robinson see that he and his colleagues are being used to launder the statements of politicians – which few voters take at face value – and give them the imprimatur of truth?

Journalists and editors who knew what was best for them were hardly likely to adopt a professional attitude after the Andrew Gilligan affair. Gilligan reported correctly that Blair's Iraq dossier had been "sexed up" on the orders of political aides in Downing Street. But errors of detail that would normally pass unnoticed were seized upon by Downing Street who eventually set up the Hutton Inquiry. Hutton criticized the BBC and vindicated Blair. Gilligan and the two most senior BBC chiefs lost their jobs, while journalists who had uncritically peddled Blair's falsehoods were untouched.

But if there was a belated measure of recognition of the lies about Iraq, the mass media was not about to put the "contradictory case" on the 9/11 events. They had reached their verdict. Reuters, the most conscientious of the US/UK newswires, held out for two and a half years, but wrote in its style-book for journalists on 22 June 2004 the following instruction:

> In stories about Al-Qaeda and the September 11 2001 attacks in the United States, we need not write that the group has been blamed for carrying them out. There is sufficient factual evidence, including several statements from Osama bin Laden asserting responsibility, for us to write that Al-Qaeda carried out the attacks or for us to use similar formulations.[19]

In fact, when the October 2004 bin Laden video appeared, it was widely and correctly (if it was not forged) described as the first clear claim of responsibility by bin Laden.

Lies are built up by a stream of new pieces of "news", manufactured by government spin doctors and reported uncritically by journalists. Later they may discover that the report is flawed, but the real news receives less prominence because the news agenda has "moved on" as editors put it. Each time, a few more of the audience are converted. The process of repetition affects journalists themselves, and, more importantly still, editors.

We have seen that Reuters' "factual evidence" consists of reports like the Barbara Olson phone call from Flight 77, an undocumented, single-sourced report, based on the word of one person in the Department of Justice, a bin Laden video no independent party has had a chance to check, or the video supposedly from Dulles Airport without any identifying marks at all. It is founded on documents like the Saudi Arabian passport that somebody apparently found in Vesey Street, while everyone else was gazing upward at the burning towers, and FBI statements about the identity of the hijackers, which in at least two cases cannot be true.

As with Iraq's WMD, media professionals, along with the public, have failed to understand that a series of half-truths does not add up to the whole truth. Even on the Iraq question, the media have shrugged off their role in one set of lies, only to adopt another set of controversial assertions. These assertions are that the conflict has nothing to do with oil, that the main goal of the occupation forces was to bring democracy to Iraq, that the WMD falsehoods were asserted in good faith, that there is a body that can accurately be described as "the Iraqi Government".

On the day of the 9/11 events, with the new narrative "terrorists attack America", the mass media repeatedly showed images of Palestinians, supposedly rejoicing over the TV Twin Towers coverage. But according to Mark Crispin Miller, a Professor of Media Studies at New York University who investigated the issue, the footage was filmed during the funeral of nine people killed the day before by Israeli authorities. He said: "to show it without explaining the background, and to show it over and over again is to make propaganda for the war machine and is irresponsible."[20]

As if the power of government were not enough, the corporate propaganda apparatus is overwhelming. Its public relations force is vast and expanding, employing about 110,000 people in the USA alone. Big PR companies own or are owned by huge global advertising agencies, such as WPP Group, with an $8.6 billion turnover and 53,000 employees, which owns PR groups Burson-Marsteller (more than seventy offices in thirty-eight countries) and Hill & Knowlton (over 100 offices in fifty-eight countries).[21]

These groups can intervene in the political process in dramatic ways. The Rendon Group PR company describes on its website that after the seizure of Kuwait by Iraq in 1991, it "established a full-scale communications operation for the government of

Kuwait, including the establishment of a production studio in London producing programming material for the exiled Kuwaiti Television". Later, the Rendon Group was paid close to $100 million for its work building the Iraq National Congress as a successor to Saddam Hussein's Baathist Party. Tim Bell, Mrs Thatcher's favourite PR man, was one of the first to be hired to promote the occupation of Iraq.

Corporations often use their financial clout as advertisers to influence the mass media's news departments. For example, a 1992 survey questioned 147 daily newspaper editors in the USA and found that 93 per cent of them admitted that advertisers had "threatened to withdraw advertising from [the] paper because of the content of the stories". The same goes for TV news, indeed corporations often advertise on mass media that they themselves own.[22]

Changes in business structures have also impinged on the media. With the exception of internet news sites, which the conventional mass media ignore, the range of independent news outlets has diminished drastically in the decade since the first Gulf War. Since then, there has been a massive consolidation in the radio and regional TV sectors in the US, while AOL Time Warner swallowed up CNN and *Time* magazine, as well as a range of smaller businesses. Organizations whose primary task a generation ago was reporting news are nowadays owned by conglomerates who control not only the US news media but large sections of film, publishing, and other communications industries.

If independent competition was more or less eliminated domestically, what about the foreign media? In the case of Iraq, major foreign governments demurred from US policy and their media reflected doubts about the WMD story. However, in the case of 9/11 most major governments were only too happy to believe the official story, at least at first, seeing it as an excuse to suspend the rule of law in dealing with their own dissident groups, or for more liberal states an opportunity to engage America with the rest of the world.

In these circumstances the power of a handful of people in the Washington newsrooms to determine the story is immense anyway, but on top of that they own the most powerful global network on the planet, the Associated Press. AP is a not-for-profit news cooperative of US newspapers and broadcasters. David Westin, president of ABC News, sits on the twenty-five member board of directors, alongside other network bosses.

AP delivers a total news service to over 5,000 radio and TV broadcasters worldwide, reaching a billion people in 120 nations, but it does more than that. It also delivers a total newsroom solution, involving news input and the computer systems to go with it. More than 3,300 broadcasters operate them in over sixty countries.

One potential snag exists for rule by corporate TV news. Inconveniently, the airwaves belong to the public, and channels are regulated by the Federal Communications Commission. It's Chairman is Michael Powell, son of General Colin Powell. Powell's salient quality as head of the agency is his apparent belief that it need not exist, since it's better to "let markets pick winners and losers". "The oppressor here is regulation," Powell said. No wonder his appointment was hailed as "an outstanding choice" by the industry.[23]

Conclusion

It is not the object of this book to promote any particular scenario concerning what happened in the 9/11 events, but even so we feel able to draw some conclusions from the evidence we have examined.

Firstly, the official account has changed dramatically as a result of the pressure from 9/11 skeptics and particularly the families of 9/11 victims. Suppose that instead of saluting Bush on TV as commander-in-chief after 9/11, Al Gore had said that Democrats had prevented such attacks for the last eight years, and that before they agreed to a "war on terror" there must be a genuine investigation into what had gone wrong?

Now we know that the investigation would have found a very different picture to the self-serving first version of the official story: Al-Qaeda succeeding not by a fiendish, rich, and professional structure but by good luck, with a plan that should have been foiled. In contrast to the statements immediately after the attacks from Bush, Blair, and Rice, we now know that the attacks were far from "unthinkable": warnings were lost, FBI HQ blocked investigations that might have aborted the attacks, and as Thomas Kean put it, senior officials failed and should be sacked.

None of this information would have come out without the intervention of skeptics. If the dissenters have contributed little else, they have established that the democratic institutions of a party of opposition and a free media both failed in the wake of the 9/11 events. In the face of media hysteria and the paralysis of the anthrax attacks, the Washington establishment endorsed without inquiry or even much debate the war plans of a man who lost the popular vote and whose key financial backer, Enron, would soon be facing charges of false accounting.

Our second conclusion, and for us the most surprising, is that on the publicly available evidence, a plot by elements of the US Government on the lines of Operation Northwoods cannot easily be ruled out. True, the Pentagon's radar reconstructions reportedly indicate the planes were not switched, and the alleged Al-Qaeda ringleaders are said by their interrogators to have confirmed the official story.

But the evidence that would rule out a Northwoods-type plan – independent scrutiny of plane parts and telephone records, the release of seized photos showing what really happened at the Pentagon – is conspicuously missing from the Kean Inquiry, while the strangely long flight paths and many technical ambiguities suggest the possibility that planes could indeed have been switched. Of course, this is a long way from proof that a Northwoods-style operation did occur, but it does illustrate the lack of the hard evidence that victims and the public are entitled to demand before they go to war.

Our third conclusion is that with the Kean Commission Report the official story of the 9/11 events is in a sorry state indeed. Half hearted attempts to answer some 9/11 skeptics without arousing the suspicions of America's 9/11 believers only highlight the gaps in its inquiry. These gaps have led to its deserved dismissal by 9/11 skeptics as the "Kean Omission".

In its attempts to explain the Pentagon's failure to follow procedures, scramble planes and intercept the rogue aircraft, the Commission asks us to believe that four planes with eight pilots were taken over by bloodthirsty hijackers armed only with knives, without even one hijack warning being made.

The Commission reports without comment that with two planes hijacked already and the Twin Towers in flames, it never occurred to the controller of the vanished Flight 77 that it might have been hijacked. It never questions why every one of the Al-Qaeda hijackers – several of whom were apparently terrorist suspects – used their own identities to enter the US and carry out the attacks, even though he recounts that Al-Qaeda had an effective passport factory in Afghanistan.

The Kean Report's shortcomings extend over a wide range of issues. Two more examples stand out. Firstly, senior and experienced FBI officers have stated on record that specific concrete investigations that might have foiled the attacks were actively blocked on orders from FBI headquarters – orders that were reaffirmed by each level of command when agents questioned them. This hugely suspicious issue is consigned to a couple of footnotes in the Commission's report.

Secondly, the Kean Commission faithfully reports the White House line that there was an unfortunate paralysis concerning all matters connected with Al-Qaeda through 2001. Top officials like Rumsfeld and Rice are uncritically taken at their word – they were preoccupied with other matters and at a loss as to what course to take in Afghanistan. The Commission seems entirely unaware of foreign media reports that, on the contrary, US diplomats were in fact making repeated threats to invade Afghanistan during the same period.

Our final conclusion is that due to the absence of solid proof for virtually any part of the official story, there are viable scenarios that involve an input from factions on both sides of the "war on terror". There is evidence for the possibility that genuine Al-Qaeda hijackers were monitored, protected, and even actively helped by US authorities and their allies in Pakistan and Saudi Arabia.

One suspect here would be alleged ringleader Khalid Sheikh Mohammed, described by the Washington neocons as an Iraqi agent and by the Kean Commission as a freelance terrorist. The Kean Commission reports that KSM worked for the Northern Alliance before he defected to their enemy, Al-Qaeda, bringing with him his plan for the 9/11 attacks. The Northern Alliance, the clearest beneficiaries of the 9/11 events, were returned to power in Afghanistan by the US-led invasion of 2001/2.

This leads to the question posed throughout history to unravel mysteries like this: who else benefited from the attacks? Osama bin Laden's Al-Qaeda has achieved two key goals: leadership of militant Islamic fundamentalism, and drawing the US into a land war in the Middle East. But equally, Washington has established a military presence at the heart of the world's remaining long-term oil reserves.

We expect that most readers will evaluate the evidence according to the attitudes they bring with them. Our impression is that those prepared to put the CIA or the Bush White House on the suspects list at all, will judge that the balance of probability is strongly in favour of some sort of criminal complicity. The September 2004 Zogby poll of New Yorkers seems to confirm this.

On the other hand, the precedent of the Watergate scandal indicates that to convince other Americans it would take an on-camera confession from Bush, Cheney or Tenet to put them on the suspects list. It was only when the Watergate tapes revealed that President Nixon – from the evidence of his own mouth – was indeed a crook and a liar (and worse still a blasphemer) that Middle America woke up.

Re-examining 9/11 is a grim affair because of the gratuitous vio-
lence of the events. In the foreground are the victims and those
who grieve for them, to whom we extend our profound sympathy.

But who is in the background? Once this seed of doubt opens,
it leads to a chillingly logical line of deception going back to
before September 2001: the falsehoods on Iraq's alleged WMD,
the false links drawn between Iraq and 9/11, the anthrax attacks,
the false statements that nobody could have imagined the 9/11
attacks might take place, and the decision announced within
hours of 9/11 to launch a war that was planned already.

The line stretches back to the 1999 neocon plans to invade
Iraq and extend US military dominance across the globe. Some
would say it stretches back to the 1970s when Cheney, Rumsfeld,
Wolfowitz, and the Committee on the Present Danger convinced
America that detente with the Soviet Union was impossible.[1]

Skeptics see another point in the line of deceit: the inaction of
the White House in the face of the summer 2001 warnings, an
inaction all the more peculiar from people who had made their
careers out of blood curdling warnings that the US was in mortal
danger. As Thomas Powers, widely respected in Washington as
the unofficial historian of the CIA, wrote in the *New York Review
of Books*, late in 2004:

> There are lots of things to do when you don't know
> exactly what to do. But the President did nothing. It
> would be hard to find words adequate to describe the full
> range and amplitude of the nothing that he did. My own
> preliminary, working explanation is that for reasons of his
> own the President decided to do nothing.[2]

Unlike Powers, most opinion formers in the English-speaking
world still accept the official story on 9/11 – at least in public.
But few of them have examined the evidence, and more evidence is needed.

Gore Vidal, an early 9/11 skeptic, was prophetic in his statement that only after a disaster in Iraq would the US/UK public seriously question 9/11. The unexpected resistance movement there focused relentless attention on the failure to find the promised weapons of mass destruction. Official admissions and media mea culpas followed. The 2004 US election was electrified by the Howard Dean insurgency, when for a few weeks it looked as if an anti-war Democrat from outside Washington might win the primaries. But what about the point at the center of the line of deceit: the 9/11 events themselves?

Already many reports have chipped away at the edges of the story and the BBC's *Power of Nightmares* series late in 2004 even debunked the Al-Qaeda myth. Court actions from 9/11 skeptics are simmering away. Thomas Kean's 9/11 Commission seems, if anything, to have backfired, fuelling more suspicion.

If the skeptics are right, the official 9/11 story depends on a continuing cover-up by the corporate media, which is being daily eroded by internet websites, foreign media, independently owned outlets, and the glaring gaps in the official story. At some point – even in Washington – fair-minded people will start to draw negative conclusions from the fact that after four years and three official inquiries the establishment was still unable to provide a plausible account backed up by hard evidence of exactly what happened.

The 9/11 Truth Movement includes people of many hues. These include outright skeptics, victims' relatives, and even 9/11 believers who just think that a genuine investigation should take place to prove to the world what happened. Like the world justice ("anti-globalization") movement, which the 9/11 events did so much to undermine, or even the movement against the Vietnam War, the 9/11 Truth Movement includes conservatives who see Washington's imperial designs as just the sort of thing the revolutionary founding fathers of the US Constitution wished to prevent.

On the other hand, those whose careers or funding depend on the goodwill of corporate America – whether they are politicians, academics, or in the media; whether they are Democrats or Republicans – are understandably unwilling to put their ultimate bosses on the 9/11 suspect list.

The demands are getting ever louder for a genuine no-holds-barred inquiry into 9/11 that is fully independent of the Washington establishment. Some are calling for a grand jury, which would have subpoena powers and could be run by suspicious prosecutors from outside Washington. Others, a re-working of a blue ribbon panel for an International Truth Commission. We support such calls wholeheartedly. Whatever you think about the facts – or absence of them – this issue is not going to go away.

References

Readers wishing to learn more about the lastest research can visit www.911revealed.co.uk, which provides details of the main online resources.

Chapter 1: The Official Story

[1] The Pentagon, too, was under pressure. On September 10 Rumsfeld admitted that "according to some estimates we cannot touch $2.3 trillion (sic) in transactions". http://www.defencelink.mil/speeches/2001/S20010910-secdef.html

[2] Thompson, op. cit.

[3] For Cheney, http://www.septembereleventh.org/newsarchive/2004-02-11-investigate.php

[4] http://www.9/11commission.gov/hearings/hearing12/jnfitzgerald_statement. pdf, *Christian Science Monitor*, 1 March 2002, http://www.csmonitor.com/2002/0301/p01s02-usmi.html

[5] CNN, 6 July 2004

[6] Hufschmid book, op. cit.

[7] http://www.zogby.com/news/ReadNews.dbm?ID=855

[8] Live on *The Westminster Hour*, BBC Radio 4, October 2001

[9] Clarke, Richard A., *Against All Enemies*, London, 2004

[10] www.scoop.co.nz/mason/stories/HL0310/S00115.html

[11] *Newsday*, 4 June 2002, Associated Press

12 http://septembereleventh.org/newsarchive/2003-12-20-pnackle.php

13 Kean Commission Report, p. 13

14 For training, http://news.bbc.co.uk/1/hi/world/south_asia/155236.stm

15 For Rumsfeld, CNN, 30 September 2002,
    http://archives.cnn.com/2002/US/09/30/sproject.irq.regime.change/

16 http://www.nydailynews.com/front/story/147141p-129811c.html

17 For Taliban, Kean Commission Report, Chapter 7

Chapter 2: Alternative Scenarios

1 See Bibliography for the key books and websites

2 *The New Pearl Harbor*, Arris Books, www.arrisbooks.com
   http://www.newamericancentury.org/, but this is a big file, see also
   www.informationclearinghouse.info/article5506.html, and
   http://www.oilempire.us/pnac.html

4 Stinnett, Robert B., *Day of Deceit: The Truth about FDR and Pearl Harbor*,
   Touchstone, 2001. For Stinnett's comments www.btinternet.com/
   ~nlpwessex/Documents/pearlharbor.html

5 www.abc.se/~pa/mar/ussmaine.html for Tonkin
   www.fair.org/media-beat/940727.html)

6 Blum, William, *Rogue State: A Guide to the World's Only Superpower*,
   London, 2001; for Guatemala, *Guardian*, 12 March 1999

7 For neocons, Seymour Hersh, *New Yorker*, 12 May 2003

8 *San Francisco Chronicle* 15 January 2004,
   http://sfgate.com/cgi-bin/article.cgi?f=/c/a/2004/01/15/MNGK14AC301.DTL

9 DSB, Summer Study on Special Operations and Joint Forces in Support of
   Counter-Terrorism, Final Outbrief, 16 August 2002 [declassified version],
   cited in Kick, R., *50 Things You're Not Supposed To Know*, 2003. William
   Arkin, *LA Times*, 27 October 2002

10 For more on these issues, and the disturbing comments of some US Left
    Wingers see www.questionsquestions.net/topics/left_gatekeepers.htm,
    http://www.publiceye.org/top_conspire.html

11 House of Representatives' Permanent Select Committee on Intelligence,
    IC21: The Intelligence Community in the 21st Century, cited in Kick, R.,
    50 Things You're Not Supposed To Know, 2003

12 Agee, Philip, *Inside the Company: CIA Diary*, London, 1975; Ostrovsky,
    Victor, *The Other Side of Deception: A Rogue Agent Exposes the Mossad's
    Secret Agenda*, New York, 1995; Marks, Howard, *Mr Nice: An Autobiography*,
    London, 1997

13 Hilton interview transcript http://www.rense.com/general57/aale.htm original
    audio at http://www.prisonplanet.tv/audio/091004hilton.mp3
    Hilton added "And I've been harassed personally to drop this suit, threatened
    [with being kicked] off the court, after 30 years on the court. I've been
    harassed by the FBI. My staff has been harassed and threatened. My office
    has been broken into . . ." His case was later reported quashed by a federal
    judge on the grounds of sovereign immunity.

14 Posner, Gerald L., *Why America Slept*, Ballantine Books, 2004.
    In an earlier book, *Case Closed*, Posner revisited the Kennedy assassination
    and decided it was carried out by Lee Harvey Oswald on his own after all. See
    http://karws.gso.uri.edu/JFK/the_critics/wrone/ Review_of_Case_Closed.html.
    For a sympathetic review of Posner, see
    http://www.atimes.com/atimes/Front_Page/EI17Aa01.html

15 http://www.forbiddentruth.net/; www.gregpalast.com

16 http://www.newyorkmetro.com/nymetro/news/sept11/features/5513/,
    www.rememberjohn.com. This does not appear to be an official site however.

Chapter 3: Flight 11: No Mayday Calls

1 CNN, 26 November 1996, http://cnn.com.ru/US/9611/25/airport.security/
   index.html; San Jose *Metro*, 2–8 January 1997

2 CNN, 14 September 2001

3 Kean Commission Report, p. 84

4 (1) for an introduction see Ray Griffin op. cit. and (2) www.standown.net,
   which makes the interesting point that pilots experiencing a comms failure
   should keep to course, and therefore the course deviations should have
   been strong evidence for hijacking.
   (4) http://www.af.mil/news/airman/1299/home2.htm, (5) James Banford op.
   cit. pp. 33–39, (6) FAA manualf quoted in Griffin p. 174 note 3, (7) chairman
   of the joint chiefs or staff instructions June 2001 ref 3610.01A, 1997 ref
   3025.15 and 1993 3025.1. These latter reference numbers will find the
   originals on Google. There has been much debate as to whether these
   instructions amount to a standown order, it appears to us they do because in
   the case of the hijacking 3025.1 does not make provision for emergency
   reactions without NMCC clearances. In any case the confusing June 2001
   memo can only have contributed to the paralysis on the day.

5 www.truthout.org/docs–2005/021705W.shtml

6 http://www.fromthewilderness.com/free/ww3/11_20_01_911murder
   Update.html

7   http://www.attackonamerica.net/jetcouldwrecknuclearnrcadmits.htm

8   Kean Commission Report, p. 37

9   http://news.bbc.co.uk/1/hi/world/americas/1556096.stm

10   *New York Observer*, 21 June, 2004 mirrored at
     inn.globalfreepress.com/modules/news/article.php?storyid=470

11   *Washington Post*, 6 May 2004

12   http://www.worldnetdaily.com/images2/faa911memoside.jpg

13   www.greatbuildings.com/www.skyscraper.org/www.sweetliberty.org/

14   http://www.framerate.net/wtc/john.shtml

15   Kean Commission Report, p. 531, and p. 72, Note 171

16   Kean Commission Report, p. 316

17   Kean Commission Report, p. 318

18   If the authorities had acted a little more effectively, the WTC death toll could
     have been lower than 1,500. By comparison, up to 100,000 Iraqi civilians
     were estimated to have been killed by mid-2004 by US-led attacks and on the
     first night of the London Blitz, 7–8 September 1940, Luftwaffe bombers killed
     430 and seriously injured 16,000 (the attacks continued for nine months).
     www.holnet.org.uk/learningzone/londonatwar/airraid/ p_theblitz.html, link,
     http://english.aljazeera.net/NR/exeres/
     66E32EAF-0E4E-4765-9339-594C323A777F.htm

19   AP report, 15 January 2002

20   Source: *New York Daily News*, 11 September 2002
     http://www.wtc-terrorattack.com/wtc-daten.htm
     Inside 9/11: What Really Happened, by the reporters, writers and editors of
     . *Der Spiegel*, St Martin's Paperbacks, 2001
     Trentini information: http://www.september11victims.com/ for a
     comprehensive victims list

21   BBC, 28 February 2003, http://news.bbc.co.uk/2/low/americas/2808599.stm
     "Wisnewski, see bibliography"

22   Kean Commission Report, Staff Statement 13

23   http://www.chiefengineer.org/article.cfm?seqnum1=1029

24   BBC correspondent Steve Evans also reported "huge explosions"
     http://www.thisisthenortheast.co.uk/the_north_east/news/attack/1209_3.html,
     Evans' quote seems to have disappeared from the BBC website

25   Paul Thompson, *Timeline People*, 12 September 2001

Chapter 4: A Second Aircraft Hits the South Tower

1 Kean Commission Report, p. 7

2 Author's Notes

3 *Guardian*, 17 October 2001

4 www.globalsecurity.org/military/facility/griffiss/htm

5 *Boston Globe,* 11 September 2002, all times and details from Paul Thompson, op. cit.

6 Pentagon op. cit., 174, pp. 115, www.pavepaws.org
   www.at.mil/factsheets/factsheet/asp?ts10=168

7 http://www.at.mil/news/airman/1203/enemy.html

8 *New York Daily News*, 11 September 2002, www.sysplan.com, www.bts.gov

Chapter 5: The Towers Collapse

1 *New York Times*, 4 August 2002

2 Kean Commission Report, Staff Statement 13, source: TCM Archives

3 www.thememoryhole.org/911/firefighter-tape.htm and
   http://www.americanfreepress.net/08_09_02/New_York_Firefighters__/
   new_york_firefighters__.html

4 http://www.usc.edu/dept/engineering/illumin/vol3issue3/wtc/page5.html

5 *New Scientist*, 12 September 2001,
   http://www.newscientist.com/news/news.jsp?id=ns99991281

6 http://www.abqjournal.com/news/aqvan09-11-01.htm
   http://emperors-clothes.com/news/albu.html

7 Ryan's letter can be found at
   http://www.911truth.org/article.php?story=20041112144051451

8 http://www.sweetliberty.org/issues/war/wag2.html is a must-read article on
   the psy-ops angle, which many 9/11 skeptics see in the events

9 http://www.vancouver.indymedia.org/news/2003/02/34507.php

10 www.enr.construction.com/news/buildings/archives/021104.asp

11 This site has a very thorough discussion of these issues
   http://911review.org/Wget/members.fortunecity.com/911/wtc/clifton.htm

12 www.tags.orgs/docs/911/911Report-317.html

13 http://www.firehouse.com/terrorist/911/magazine/gz/hayden.html

14 Source for experts: *How the Towers Collapsed* – Discovery Channel

15 *Newsday* "Expert, WTC Probe Under Funded" – 11 January 2002

16 *American Free Press*, 27 May 2002

17 *Baltimore Sun*, 3 January 2002

18 For an interesting overview and lead to the various sources, http://www.truth-now.com/911/pullwtc/

19 http://www.abc.net.au/news/features/stories/s373834.html
www.freerepublic.com/focus/news/527722/posts)

20 Salon.com, Christopher Ketcham, 19 September 2001

21 "Below Ground Zero, Silver and Gold", New York Times, 1 November 2001

22 *National Real Estate Investor*, 19 November 2001

23 http://www.datarecovery-europe.com/presse/26_09_02.htm

24 *A History of Waste Management In New York City*, link,
http://www.johnmccrory.com/bags/history/history2.html

25 *Village Voice*, 28 November 2001

26 "Why the Corporate Invasion of Iraq Must be Stopped" by CorpWatch, Global
Exchange, Public Citizen, Collaborative Report, 5 June 2003

27 http://www.metropulse.com/dir_zine/dir_2003/1337/t_cover.html

28 US Corps of Engineers' report,
http://www.hq.usace.army.mil/History/9-11%20Highlights.htm

29 Source: AP Richard Pyle, 23 February 2002,
Link: http://www.detnews.com/2002/nation/0202/24/a09-425213.html,
Source: *New York Daily News*, 8 June 2002

30 AP, Richard Pyle, 23 February 2002, *NYT*, 8 June 2002, *New York Daily News*,
9 June 2002

Chapter 6: Flight 77: Shrouded in Mystery

1 AP, 22 July 2004, http://foi.missouri.edu/terrorintelligence/survvideo.html

2 Kean Commission Report, p. 460, Note 142, Note 144

3 Op. cit.

4 Kean Commission Report, Staff Report 17,
http://www.911review.org/Wiki/Flight77TowerConversations.shtml

5 military.com, *Washington Post*, 16 September 2001 or
http://www.911review.org/Wget/www.washingtonpost.com/ac2/
wp-dyn/A38407-2001Sep15

6 Kean Commission Report, Chapter 1

7   Ray Griffin, op. cit.

8   Dr Thomas Olsted, *Sierra Times*, 06/07/03
    Link: http://www.sierratimes.com/03/images/foia/foia-10001.jpg,
    http://www.dcmilitary.com/army/pentagram/6_47/local_news/12303-1.html,
    LA Times, 27 September 2001

9   *LA Times*, 27 September 2001, cited at http://www.jdupree.com/terror.html

10 http://www.nylawyer.com/news/01/09/091701i.html, 17 September 2001

11 http://billstclair.com/911timeline/2002/telegraph030502.html

12 Pentagon Renovation Program, link, http://www.disaster-resource.com/content_page/fac104.shtml

13 Op. cit., above

14 *The Virginian Pilot*, 10 September 2002,
    www.hamptonroads.com/pilotonline/special/911

15 www.amec.com

16 AMEC press release, www.realtimetraders.com, 3 December 2004, Terry Macalister, *Guardian*, 25 March 2004, Corpwatch War Profiteers

17 http://911review.org/Wiki/PentagonAttackDamage.shtml
    http://www.architectureweek.com/2003/0212/news_1-1.html

18 Kean Commission Report, p. 315

19 *Annual Status Report to Congress*, 3 January 2002

20 http://www.total911.info/2005/02/video-cnn-reported-no-plane-hit.html
    http://thewebfairy.com/911/pentagon/27_1-mcintyre.swf
    http://macbrussell.com/9-11/dear%20world%watcher.html

21 Op. cit.

22 911review.org/wiki/PentagonAttackWitnessesBlast/shtml

23 http://www.whitehouse.gov/news/releases/2001/11/20011110-3.html

24 http://news.nationalgeographic.com/news/2001/12/1211_wirepentagon.html

25 http://www.airdisaster.com/cgi_bin/view_details.cgi?date=09112001&veg=N644A

26 http://thewebfairy.com/killtown/flight77/witnesses.html for a selection

27 Marrs op. cit., p. 26

28 For Faram discussion with skeptic see
    http://www.apfn.net/messageboard/9-21-02/discussion.cgi.86.shtml

29 Ray Griffin, op. cit.

30 www.americanhistory.si.edu/september11/collection/supporting.asp?ID=30

31 www.usmedicine.com/article.cfm?articleID=384&issueID=38

32 www.af.mil/news/Apr2002/n20020415_0585.shtml

33 *Scientific American*, September 2000,
http://archives.cnn.com/2001/US/09/14/investigation.terrorism/
http://www.defenselink.mil/news/Sep2001/n09142001_200109142.html

Chapter 7: Flight 93

1 Kean Commission Report, p. 245

2 Kean Commission Report, p. 456, Note 74

3 Kean Commission Report, p. 11

4 Kean Commission Report, p. 10

5 Kean Commission Report, Staff Report 17,
http://sf.indymedia.org/news/2004/06/1697037.php

6 Kean Commission, Hearing 2

7 http://inn.globalfreepress.com/modules/news/article.php?storyid=323

8 *Pittsburgh Post-Gazette*, 28 October 2001, *Newsweek*, 26 November 2001,
Newsweek's link has expired but a shortened version is at
www.dailyherald.com/special/waronterrorism/story.asp?intID=37225488

9 Kean Commission Report, pp. 30–31

10 http://www.post-gazette.com/headlines/20010912crashnat2p2.asp

11 http://www.cbsnews.com/stories/2003/08/08/attack/main567260.shtml

12 Kean Commission Report, p. 33

13 Richard Wallace, *Daily Mirror*, link, http://www.mirror.co.uk/news/allnews/
page.cfm?objectid=12192317&method=full&siteid=50143

14 *Independent*, 13 August 2002

Chapter 8: The Alleged Hijackers

1 For CIA man, *Christian Science Monitor*, 21 June 2004
http://www.csmonitor.com/2004/0621/dailyUpdate.html, for tape, MSNBC, 30
October 2004 http://msnbc.msn.com/id/6363306/

2 http://www.washingtonpost.com/wp-srv/national/dotmil/arkin020199.htm,
and also *New York Times*, 1/8/2001, which seems to refer to a different
system developed by AT@T

3   For Musharraf, http://edition.cnn.com/2002/WORLD/asiapcf/south/01/18/
     gen.musharraf.binladen/, for his state of health,
     http://www.cnn.com/2002/HEALTH/01/21/gupta.otsc/index.html,
     for death notice, http://www.welfarestate.com/binladen/funeral/

4   For a listing of bin Laden statements see http://www.robert-
     fisk.com/understanding_enemy.htm, for skeptics,
     www.whatreallyhappened.com/osamatape.html, for official transcript,
     www.defenselink.mil/news/Dec2001/d20011213ubl.pdf

5   For second tape, http://news.bbc.co.uk/2/hi/middle_east/2526309.stm
     http://www.cbsnews.com/stories/2002/11/12/attack/main529066.shtml

6   *Miami Herald*, 30 April 2002
     http://www.miami.com/mld/miamiherald/3163998.htm

7   *Masterminds of Terror* by Yosri Fouda and Nick Fielding, Arcade Publishing
     2002

8   The two key sources for this topic are
     http://cooperativeresearch.org/timeline/main/essayksmcapture.html
     which cites *Asia Times* 30 October 2002 for the claim KSM is dead and
     Financial Times 11 September 2002 for the expert's opinion on Fouda's
     interview. In cited *Guardian* article (4 March 2003) Fouda mentions a "slip of
     the tongue" by KSM who implies at one point OBL is already dead.
     The other source is
     http://onlinejournal.com/Special_Reports/121603Kupferberg/
     121603kupferberg.html
     which has a discussion of Fouda's change of the interview date, with an
     apparent quote from Fouda himself.

9   http://www.dailyexcelsior.com/01sep29/inter.htm citing Reuters

10 Dan Eggen, George Lardner Jr. and Susan Schmidt, *Washington Post*, 20
     September 2001

11 For flight manifests, see for instance, Von Buelow, op. cit., or in English,
     http://www.globalresearch.ca/articles/DAV407A.html

12 http://news.bbc.co.uk/1/hi/world/middle_east/1558669.stm

13 23 September 2001,
     http://www.portal.telegraph.co.uk/news/main.jhtml?xml=/news/2001/09/23/w
     iden23.xml

14 CNN, 13 September 2004
     archives.cnn.com/2001/US/09/12/investigation.terrorism/

15 For autopsy reports, http://www.sierratimes.com/03/07/02/article_tro.htm

[16] http://www.onlinejournal.com/Special_Reports/073104Burns/073104burns.html, for the new system, http://www.infowars.com/transcripts/springman.htm, Springman also gave an interview to the BBC's *Newsnight*

[17] *National Review*, 6/10/2004, http://www.nationalreview.com/mowbray/mowbray100902.asp

[18] *Knight Ridder* quoted at http://www.inthesetimes.com/site/main/article/615/

[19] *New York Observer*, quoted at http://www.inthesetimes.com/site/main/article/615/

[20] *Focus*, quoted in Thompson, op. cit.

[21] For quote, http://www.oudaily.com/vnews/display.v/ART/2002/01/24/3fd758936f255?in_archive=1

[22] Tami Watson, "CIA Officer: Terrorism Is Still a Threat", The Norman Transcript, 12 February 2002, p. 1 quoted at http://members.aol.com/mpwright9/sting.html

[23] For Edger at HQ: *Washington Times*, 8/1/95 section a4 quoted at http://spot.acorn.net/jfkplace/03/RM/RM.cohen-aug http://www.news-star.com/stories/14001/spe.20.shtml

[24] Wisnewski, op. cit. – this story has been extensively covered in the mainstream German media, e.g. *Frankfurter Rundschau*, 12 and 13 August 2004

[25] www.whitehouse.gov/response/faq-what.html

[26] www.madcowprod.com/, Hopsicker has written two books available through his website – he is also an established TV producer

[27] Hopsicker, op. cit.

[28] Kean Commission Report, Chapter 7, Note 190

[29] *Los Angeles Times*, 23 October 2001, on the web at http://www.sun-sentinel.com/news/local/southflorida/sns-worldtrade-jarrah-lat.story, though by 2003 the *LA Times* had adopted a completely different tone in discussing the letter – see billstclair.com/911timeline/2003/latimes012703.html

[30] www.cnn.com/2002/US/08/01/cia.hijacker

[31] Kean Commission Report, Chapter 5, Note 97

[32] Leading neocon James S. Robbins, in a 2002 article denouncing 9/11 skeptics as akin to holocaust deniers, made the claim that he had personally seen Flight 77 "diving in at an unrecoverable angle" – see http://www.nationalreview.com/robbins/robbins040902.asp

[33] 8.6.2002, http://news.bbc.co.uk/2/hi/programmes/
from_our_own_correspondent/2033791.stm,
Kean mentions only that the hotel is in Herndon

[34] The *Washington Post* quoted in *The Cape Cod Times*, 21 October 2001, at
http://www.whatreallyhappened.com/hanjour_history.html

[35] Kean Commission Report, Chapter 7

[36] Kean Commission Report, Chapter 7, Note 170 – it appears from Kean's
account, buried in a footnote, that the Maryland story may not even have
surfaced until 2004

[37] Kean Commission Report, p. 532, Note 191

[38] http://www.worldnetdaily.com/news/article.asp?ARTICLE_ID=37781

[39] www.cooperativeresearch.org/timeline/main/randyglass.html

[40] http://www.lectlaw.com/files/cur46.htm

[41] The *New York Times* account, 3 August 1993, and Mossad agent go through
complete timeline at http://www.cooperativeresearch.org

[42] http://www.newyorker.com/fact/content/?020128fa_FACT, Seymour Hersh for
Kunduz, *Newsweek*, 26 August 2002 for atrocities

[43] *Le Nouvel Observateur*, Paris, 15–21 January 1998, posted at
globalresearch.ca 15 October 2001

[44] *Observer*, 11/11/02, (http://www.usatoday.com/news/world/2003-03-02-
alqaeda-list_x.htm, but note that this is a different man to Abu-faraj Al-Liby,
now described as overall AQ operations chief

[45] For a well-sourced overview of these issues see Chris Floyd, *Moscow Times*, 18
February 2005 copied at www.informationclearinghouse.info/article8110.htm

[46] http://avantgo.thetimes.co.uk/services/avantgo/article/0,,1150429,00.html
http://www.expatica.com/source/site_article.asp?subchannel_id=81&story_id
=8393 10 June 2004

[47] Edith Regalado, 9 July 2002, *Philippine Star*, archived at
http://www.philstar.com,
http://www.defendsison.be/archive/pages/0303/030309Fake.html

[48] *The Nation*, 1 September 2003,
http://www.thenation.com/doc.mhtml%3Fi=20030901&s=klein

[49] *Vanity Fair*, 8 December 2001, cited e.g. at
http://www.sudanembassy.org/default.asp?page=viewstory&id=66

[50] *Le Figaro*, 31 October 2001, translated at
http://www.scoop.co.nz/mason/stories/HL0111/S00018.htm

51 CBS, 28 January 2002, cited at http://globalresearch.ca/articles/CHO311A.html

52 *Observer* 25 November 2001, p. 17

53 http://www.csmonitor.com/2001/1213/p1s1-wosc.html

54 http://www.counterpunch.org/cockburn11012004.html, Counterpunch does not generally endorse 9/11 skepticism beyond this LIHOP accusation of criminal negligence

Chapter 9: Paralysis at the FBI

1 For August memo, Kean Commission Report

2 http://www.fromthewilderness.com/free/ww3/051602_liewontstand.html

3 FA2 11 September 2001 http://derstandardrat/?url=/?id=1631377

4 Der Standard op. cit.

5 http://www.gordonthomas.ie/104.html

6 http://www.msnbc.msn.com/id/4619346/

7 See e.g. Kean, source for Watson Knut Royce and Tom Brune, *Newsday*, 10 April 2004

8 Royce and Brune, ibid.

9 http://www.pbs.org/newshour/bb/white_house/Jan–June04/oath.04–08.html

10 Alan Elsner, Reuters, Washington, April 2004

11 Ahmed, Nafeez Mosaddeq, *The War on Freedom*, http://www.mediamonitors.net/mosaddeq36.html

12 Griffin, op. cit., quoting *Fortune*, 22 May 2002, see also Kean Staff Statement 11

13 UPI, 30 May 2002, cited in Griffin, p. 83, http://www.truthout.org/docs_02/08.03B.jvb.wright.htm

14 http://news.bbc.co.uk/2/hi/business/4204065.stm

15 Congressional Intelligence Committee, cited in Griffin, p. 83

16 Kean Commission Report, Chapter 8, Note 81

17 Rowley's memo was widely published – we use the *Time* magazine website version, which includes important footnotes

18 It has been stated frequently – although we have not found an original source for this – that the contents of his laptop would have betrayed the plan for the 9/11 events

[19] The Kean Commission Report's only mention of the Rowley memo (Staff Statement 11) it blames the UK for failing to respond to a request for information on Moussaoui. They fail to mention the information from France.

[20] *New York Times*, 15 April 2004

[21] http://www.salon.com/politics/feature/2002/06/08/frasca/index_np.html

[22] http://www.startribune.com/dynamic/story.php?template=print_a&story=5163680

Chapter 10: Line of Deceit

[1] *Guardian*, 6 September 2003

[2] *Toronto Star*, 19 January 2003

[3] *Sunday Telegraph*, 14 December 1997
http://www.rememberjohn.com/Oilbarons.html

[4] Suskind, Ron, *The Price of Loyalty*, Simon & Schuster, 2004. This book was informed by a large archive of current papers provided by O'Neill when he was fired by Bush as Treasury Secretary

[5] BBC, 18 September 2001,
http://news.bbc.co.uk/1/hi/world/south_asia/1550366.stm, for Bridas,
http://www.worldpress.org/specials/pp/pipeline_timeline.htm

[6] www.whitehouse.gov/news/releases/2001/05/print/02010508.html
http://archives.cnn.com/2001/ALLPOLITICS/05108/senate.terrorism.02

[7] http://www.scoop.co.nz/mason/stories/WO0406/S00098.htm

[8] *Guardian*, 10/9/2001,
http://www.guardian.co.uk/Archive/Article/0,4273,4253580,00.html

[9] Woodward, op. cit.

[10] *Guardian*, September 12 2001

[11] www.btinternet.com/~nlpwessex/Documents/WATomarsheikhgate.htm

[12] *Newsweek*, quoted at
http://www.totse.com/en/conspiracy/institutional_analysis/166506.html

[13] The original *Times of India* report, as well as the *Wall Street Journal* summary of it is now extremely hard to find on the web, but the *Times of India* recapitulated it an article to be found at
http://timesofindia.indiatimes.com/cms.dll/html/uncomp/articleshow?msid=107432, ref for all reports,
http://www.globalresearch.ca/articles/KUP209A.html

[14] http://www.counterpunch.com/boyle0425.html

[15] CBS News, 20 July 2004

[16] ABC News, 4 April 2002, quoted at http://www.911dossier.co.uk/ax02.html

[17] http://www.corpwatch.org/article.php?id=11336

[18] http://progressivetrail.org/articles/040813Whitney.shtml

[19] Published on the Reuters intranet on 22 June 2004

[20] Paul Thompson, op. cit., AFP, 18 September 2001, *Australian*, 27 September 2001

[21] The websites of the various corporations

[22] http://www.cni.org/Hforums/roundtable/1995–02/0040.html
Editor and Publisher 16 January 1993, p. 28

[23] TheStandard.com, 6/5/01, *Washington Post*, 23 January 2001, *Communications Daily*, 23 January 2001

Conclusion

[1] See for instance *The Power of Nightmares* produced for the BBC by Adam Curtis
http://news.bbc.co.uk/l/hi/programmes/3951615.stm

[2] http://www.nybooks.com/articles/17637

Bibliography

Ahmed, Nafeez Mosaddeq and Leonard, John, *The War on Freedom: How and Why America Was Attacked on 9/11*, Tree of Life Publications, 2002

Alterman, Eric, *When Presidents Lie: a History of Official Deception and Its Consequences*, Penguin USA, 2004

Bamford, James, *A Pretext for War: 9/11, Iraq, and the Abuse of America's Intelligence Agencies*, Doubleday, 2004

Brisard, Jean-Charles, Dasquie, Guillaume, and Madsen, Wayne, *Forbidden Truth: US-Taliban Secret Oil Diplomacy, Saudi Arabia and the Failed Search for bin Laden*, Thunder's Mouth Press, 2002

Brzezinski, Matthew, *Fortress America: on the Front Lines of Homeland Security, an Inside Look at the Coming Surveillance State*, Bantam Doubleday Dell, 2004

Cardeñosa, Bruno, *11-S Historia de Una Infamia*, Corona Borealis, 2003

Chomsky, Noam, *9-11*, Seven Stories Press, 2001

Chomsky, Noam, *Hegemony or Survival*, Henry Holt & Co, 2004

Clarke, Richard A., *Against All Enemies*, Free Press, 2004

Griffin, David Ray, *The New Pearl Harbor: Disturbing Questions about the Bush Administration and 9/11*, Arris, 2004

Griffin, David Ray, *The 9/11 Commission Report: Omissions and Distortions*, Interlink, 2004

Hersh, Seymour M., *Chain of Command: the Road From 9/11 to Abu Ghraib*, HarperCollins, 2004

Hufschmid, Eric, *Painful Questions: an analysis of the September 11th Attack* (order through http://www.erichufschmid.net/)

Der Spiegel, et al., *Inside 9/11: What Really Happened*, St Martins Paperbacks, 2001

Klevemen, Lutz, *The New Great Game: Blood and Oil in Central Asia*, Grove Press, 2004

Krugman, Paul, *The Great Unravelling: From Boom to Bust in Three Scandalous Years*, Penguin, 2004

McQuaig, Linda, *It's the Crude, Dude: War, Business and the Fight for the Planet*, Doubleday Canada, 2004

Marr, Jim, *Inside Job, Unmasking the 9/11 Conspiracies*, Origin Press, 2004

Meyssan, Thierry, *Pentagate*, Carnot Publishing, 2002

Meyssan, Thierry, *9/11: the Big Lie*, Carnot Books USA, 2003

Moore, Michael, *The Official Fahrenheit 9/11 Reader*, Simon & Schuster, 2004

National Commission on Terrorist Attacks Upon the United States, *The 9/11 Commission Report: the Final Report of the National Commission on Terrorist Attacks Upon the United States*, St Martins Press, 2004

Raimondo, Justin, *Terror Enigma: 9/11 and the Israeli Connection*, Universe Inc., 2003

Ruppert, Michael C., *Crossing the Rubicon: 9/11 and the Decline of the American Empire at the End of the Age of Oil*, New Society Publishers, 2004

Strasser, Stephen, et al., *The 9/11 Investigations: Staff Reports of the 9/11 Commission: Excerpts from the House-Senate Joint Inquiry Report on 9/11: Testimony from Fourteen Key Witnesses*, Public Affairs Reports, 2004

Thompson, Paul, Center for Cooperative Research, *The Terror Timeline, Year by Year, Day by Day, Minute by Minute: a Comprehensive Chronicle of the Road to 9/11 and America's Response*, Regan Books, 2004

Von Beulow, Andreas, *Die CIA und der 11 September*, Piper, Munich, 2003

Wisnewski, Gerhard, *Mythos 9/11: Der Wahrheit auf der Spur*, Knaur, Munich, 2004

Woodward, Bob, *Plan of Attack*, Simon & Schuster, 2004

Websites

www.phsics911.org features research papers by scientists like A. K. Dewdney

911visibility.org

global research

911Truth.org

911Dossier

Authors' Notes

Inverted Commas

There is no universal transliteration system for names in Arabic, so our rendering of names may vary from other writers. As there is uncertainty over the identities of the alleged hijackers, and the nature of "Al-Qaeda", we should, in principle, put the names in inverted commas throughout, but we feel this would be clumsy. Similarly, expressions like "alleged" are used less often than logic would dictate.

References

It would have taken a great deal of space to reference every fact that we cite, so we have made judgments over what is well-known. Inevitably, readers new to this subject may find information for which we fail to give a source. Normally a Google search on two or three keywords will raise more details.

Nine/Eleven Skeptic Writers

We are hugely indebted to the often unpaid researches of 9/11 skeptics who have grown from a small band almost into a social movement. Nine/Eleven skeptics now have their own factions and tendencies. Especial praise is due to Nafeez Mossaddeq Ahmed, who wrote the seminal *The War on Freedom* within a few months of the attacks. It is measure of the strength of the skeptic case that most of his questions are still at the center of the skeptic case as we go to print.

Inside Trades

Our aim has been to deliver a broad survey of the evidence. Such a major event leaves a huge footprint from photos of the Pentagon to FBI reports, and there are inevitably areas we fail to address. We have not attempted to investigate the insider share trades. It is hard to see, for example, why one speculator seems to have left large winnings unclaimed. The Kean Commission gives the subject little mention and states, without evidence, that they have found reasons (e.g. a stockbroker's newsletter) for the strange patterns. However, it is tricky to estimate the statistical probabilities, and any culprits are hiding behind a strong shield of banking secrecy.

Methodology

There is a general objection to 9/11 skepticism. Skeptics, it is argued, collectively do a massive search for oddities and coincidences, confusing these with proof. However, we have included only evidence that bears on the key parts of the story: the hijackings, the hijackers, the official responses, and the physical evidence and eyewitnesses at the WTC and Pentagon.

An investigation like this has three logical stages, collecting the evidence, drawing up the suspects list and then deciding which story stands up best. Given that virtually any single piece of evidence can be explained away (eg. as a coincidence), the fact that there is no irrefutable smoking gun or on-record confession is no reason to leave a suspect off the list. As author Ray Griffin (op. cit.) puts it, the nature of the evidence for US collusion in the 9/11 attacks is cumulative – if one piece of evidence collapses it does not automatically discredit the rest. Skeptics say that 9/11 believers are often confused on the basic question: are the people in the US Goverment on the suspect list or not? They argue that for various reasons (Northwoods, cui bono, line of deceit etc.) they should be. Then the issue becomes, not is this or that piece of evidence refutable, but how likely the explanations are, how many coincidences are too many?